CULTURAL LITERACY

FOR THE COMMON CORE

6

STEPS TO

POWERFUL,

PRACTICAL

INSTRUCTION

FOR ALL

LEARNERS

BONNIE M. DAVIS

Solution Tree | Press
a division of
Solution Tree

Copyright © 2014 by Solution Tree Press

Materials appearing here are copyrighted. All rights are reserved. No part of this book may be reproduced or transmitted in any form or by any means (electronic, photocopying, recording, or otherwise) without prior written permission of the publisher.

555 North Morton Street
Bloomington, IN 47404
800.733.6786 (toll free) / 812.336.7700
FAX: 812.336.7790
email: info@solution-tree.com
solution-tree.com

Visit **go.solution-tree.com/instruction** to access materials related to this book.

Printed in the United States of America

18 17 16 15 14   1 2 3 4 5

Library of Congress Cataloging-in-Publication Data

Davis, Bonnie M.

  Cultural literacy for the common core : six steps to powerful, practical instruction for all learners / Bonnie M. Davis.

       pages cm.

  Includes bibliographical references and index.

  ISBN 978-1-936764-40-2 (perfect bound : alk. paper) 1. Multicultural education-- United States. 2. Culturally relevant pedagogy. 3. Education--Standards--United States. 4. Educational equalization--United States. I. Title.

  LC1099.3.D394 2014

  370.117--dc23

2014016327

Solution Tree
Jeffrey C. Jones, CEO
Edmund M. Ackerman, President

Solution Tree Press
President: Douglas M. Rife
Editorial Director: Lesley Bolton
Managing Production Editor: Caroline Weiss
Senior Production Editor: Suzanne Kraszewski
Proofreader: Sarah Payne-Mills
Cover and Text Designer: Rian Anderson
Text Compositor: Rachel Smith

As long as we inhabit a universe made homogeneous by our refusal to admit otherness, we can maintain the illusion that we possess the truth about ourselves and the world—after all, there is no "other" to challenge us!

—Parker Palmer

This book is dedicated to Principal Todd Benben and the staff at North Glendale Elementary School, who possess the courage to admit otherness and continue to learn and grow in collaborative conversations.

ACKNOWLEDGMENTS

Solution Tree Press would like to thank the following reviewers:

Debbie Anderson
Librarian, Social Studies Teacher, and
    Professional Developer
Waiakea Intermediate School
Hilo, Hawaii

Darnell Fine
Sixth- and Seventh-Grade Humanities
    Teacher and K–8 Multicultural
    Coordinator
Atlanta Neighborhood Charter
    School
Atlanta, Georgia

Sharroky Hollie
Associate Professor, Department of
    Teacher Education
California State University,
    Dominguez Hills
Carson, California

Noni M. Reis
Professor, Department of Educational
    Leadership
Connie L. Lurie College of Education
San José State University
San José, California

Scott Thomas
Executive Director
Magnet Schools of America
Washington, DC

Ava Maria Whittemore
Minority Achievement Coordinator
Office of Education That Is Multicultural
Frederick County Public Schools
Frederick, Maryland

TABLE OF CONTENTS

ABOUT THE AUTHOR

Bonnie M. Davis, PhD, is a veteran teacher of more than forty years who is passionate about education. She has taught in middle schools, high schools, universities, homeless shelters, and a men's prison. Bonnie is the recipient of numerous awards, including Teacher of the Year, the Governor's Award for Excellence in Teaching, the Anti-Defamation League's World of Difference Community Service Award, and the 2012 Educational Innovator Award.

Bonnie's publications include *How to Teach Students Who Don't Look Like You: Culturally Responsive Teaching Strategies, Second Edition*; *How to Coach Teachers Who Don't Think Like You: Using Literacy Strategies to Coach Across Content Areas*; *The Biracial and Multiracial Student Experience: A Journey to Racial Literacy*; and *Creating Culturally Considerate Schools: Educating Without Bias* with coauthor Kim L. Anderson. Other publications include *Culture* and *Practice* from the *Equity 101* book series with coauthor Curtis Linton and numerous articles on diversity and literacy instruction.

Bonnie has presented at several national conferences. She was a keynote speaker at the School Improvement 2012 Innovation Summit and is a featured educator in the PD360 Online Professional Development Video Series. She provides professional development services to districts across the United States, giving keynotes, workshops, and ongoing support through her consulting firm, Educating for Change. She received her bachelor's degree in education, her master's in English, her master's in communications, and her doctorate in English.

To book Bonnie for professional development, contact pd@solution-tree.com.

FOREWORD
By Mary Kim Schreck

To build independent learners at every age and level who are inquisitive, thoughtful self-starters driven by passion, we need to empower them so they are confident enough to take delight in and responsibility for their own learning growth. This is the hope we have when implementing the Common Core State Standards (CCSS). Before this can become a reality, we in the education community need to encourage educators to become inquisitive, thoughtful self-starters by empowering them to take responsibility for their own teaching and learning. And, we need to back them when they do just that. The Common Core is about nurturing critical thinking. Teachers cannot nurture critical thinking if compliance is rewarded over innovative, dynamic planning. Robyn Jackson (2013), in her newsletter *Mindsteps*, articulates this belief when she reflects:

> It saddens me so much to see teachers who are smart and passionate and committed to their students stop thinking, and feeling, and believing when they sit down to plan. Planning should be one of the most exciting parts of our jobs and yet we have managed to suck all of the joy out of it in the name of our templates, and forms, and SWBAT-speak [students will be able to]. We've forgotten what planning should be and made it a paperwork task, another hoop we have to jump through, a burden we must bear.

The six-step framework for cultural literacy for the Common Core that Bonnie Davis presents in this book is a welcome antidote to this dualistic approach to teaching in today's classrooms. From years of classroom experience as well as consulting experiences, Bonnie knows that it's not until teachers reconnect with their passion, their history, their willingness to be learners themselves that they can bring out the best in their students with high-quality, rigorous learning to prepare the students for a robust future in a globally literate environment.

Throughout *Cultural Literacy for the Common Core: Six Steps to Powerful, Practical Instruction for All Learners*, you will be energized and deeply motivated by the clear focus on the student as the center of educators' efforts. The Common Core serves as a masterful vehicle to this end. These standards have tremendous benefits to offer our educational system, despite some flaws in interpretation and implementation, a bumpy transition from paper and pencil to digital testing platforms, and initial assessment results that have caused some to question their dedication to the standards. The Common Core levels the playing field. Students who have often been intellectually segregated by a different set of rules, materials, and opportunities than their wealthier suburban counterparts will be able to climb out of the gap through the Common Core's insistence on rigor that is text based and not totally dependent on a student's prior knowledge (or lack of prior knowledge) and grow and flourish.

These shifts are worth the effort in and of themselves. More significantly, the Common Core can rekindle a strong and genuine passion for both learning and teaching in every classroom—a rebirth in respect and esteem for deep and thoughtful, unbiased thinking. Instead of the blind fidelity to scripted programs that demote the teaching profession to the role of formula followers and test-prep administers, we will see a resurgence of concern for individualized, creative planning. We should see a renewed authentic sense of curiosity—the genuine sign of engagement—in our students. Bonnie and I both acknowledge the joy we experienced as teachers when creating lessons that were fresh, current, and appropriate for our students as the goal—rather than planning for a classroom in which a generic student is outlined in a generic manual as the subject of instruction. As teachers, our lessons and units were works of love and expertise—built to stretch young minds and grab their curiosity.

We practiced the art of collaboration before it became formalized into the professional learning community model. We recognized that this co-creative experience yielded richer material, technique, and job satisfaction, fueling passion and energy in ourselves, our colleagues, and in the minds and imaginations of our young students. This is the environment that Bonnie is hoping the Common Core State Standards will produce and sustain. This is the vantage point from which she writes. This atmosphere will break the chains that watered-down textbook materials have forged over the years. By trying to please political groups and avoid anything controversial, our textbooks have become wastelands of boring reading that have turned off generation after generation of learners to the point that we are facing a real crisis of nonreading and nonthinking students. The Common Core and its emphasis on complexity, argument, and using multiple and varied texts should free up the classroom teacher from this paralysis. Indeed, you can't have critical thinking and well-crafted arguments *without dealing with controversy.* If we have nothing to disagree over, if the materials we are forced to use have been cleansed of all ambiguity, what do we have to talk about? Make claims about? Use as evidence to back up our statements? If we demand—as the Common Core repeatedly does—evidence and research and primary documents from our students, then no single political party will be able to write our history books or select our poetry and purposely leave out whole groups of a culturally diverse nation from its students' study materials. *Cultural Literacy for the Common Core: Six Steps to Powerful, Practical Instruction for All Learners* helps wrap the Common Core in a blanket of cultural insight and divergence that will help teachers begin to awaken the desire of all students to join the community of learners that will shape the future.

Educators must seek a balance when aligning with the Common Core—a stronger emphasis on disciplining the mind along with a stronger emphasis on allowing ourselves to dwell on essential questions and universal concepts. These have slowly eroded in the existing educational process. Educators fuse the education of heart and mind when achieving this balance. This book integrates strong shifts to higher-order thinking, talking, writing, and listening with the higher dictates of the human spirit and vision. Those who try to swing the system too far to the critical-thinking side of the pendulum while cautioning not to probe the world of feelings, personal understandings, narratives, and the powerful river of emotion are not aiming for balance. Don't listen too long to them. As Martin Luther King Jr. (1947) would remind us, "Education which stops with efficiency may prove the greatest menace to society. The most dangerous criminal may be the man gifted with reason, but with no morals." We have enough of such men in our lives already.

The fruit of Bonnie's efforts, *Cultural Literacy for the Common Core: Six Steps to Powerful, Practical Instruction for All Learners,* strives to elevate all students to their highest potential no matter their color, language, culture, size, shape, locality, origins, religious affiliation, background, or other such way to slice and dice people into categories. Her work is about *balance.* This book is an uncommonly brilliant offering to the growing collection of materials written to help educators move forward in their implementation of the Common Core State Standards.

INTRODUCTION

The Six-Step Framework

Those teachers who are students of their own impact are the teachers who are the most influential in raising students' achievement.

John Hattie

As educators, how do we become students of our own impact? How do we learn about the effects we are having on learners in our classrooms? John Hattie (2012), author of *Visible Learning for Teachers: Maximizing Impact on Learning*, shares with us a way to do exactly that; he suggests we shift our mind frame—that we become students while supporting our students in becoming their own teachers. Teachers and students participate together as learners. When we do this, we reflect on and evaluate what we do in classrooms. We question ourselves. We engage in what Hattie (2012) calls "visible teaching and learning," which occurs when "learning is the explicit and transparent goal, when it is appropriately challenging, and when the teacher and the student both (in their various ways) seek to ascertain whether and to what degree the challenging goal is attained" (pp. 17–18).

This is a major shift in focus for many educators. No longer the "sage on the stage," teachers now partner with students to learn together. Hattie (2012) points out that it is the "specific mind frames that teachers have about their role—and most critically a mind frame within which they ask themselves about the effect that they are having on student learning" (p. 18) that makes the difference in the classroom. He asks us to see ourselves as evaluators of our efforts on students.

Fortunately, this approach fits perfectly with the Common Core State Standards and the shifts in instructional practice required to implement them. As Mary Kim Schreck states in the foreword to this book, the CCSS are a "masterful vehicle" to increase rigor and level the playing field for all learners. The standards also offer new opportunities for teacher creativity and passion and guide us away from scripted lessons that shut down critical thinking and joy in learning. Instead, teachers now can search for primary texts and materials that engage and connect with students and their cultures.

Engaging learners' cultures can be an exciting venture for educators, and in this book, there are many suggestions on how to do just that—to become culturally literate. Being *culturally literate* means having an awareness of one's own culture as well as the cultures of others. It requires a continuous journey to learn what we don't know—about our own cultural practices and the practices of others—and the embedding of culturally responsive instructional practices within our own teaching practice. Culturally responsive instructional practices norm differences and support every student as a unique individual whose voice is an honored and valued part of the classroom. This creates a classroom climate conducive to the implementation of the Common Core standards.

Although the CCSS attempt to address different cultures by emphasizing writings by diverse authors, they were never intended to dictate the culturally responsive pedagogy needed for today's learners in 21st century classrooms. What is culturally responsive pedagogy? Choosing authors from different backgrounds to read in our classrooms? That is one aspect of being a culturally responsive teacher. Culturally responsive pedagogy, however, embraces much more than that strategy, positive as it is. *Culturally responsive pedagogy* occurs when we make all learners visible in the classroom and give them a voice; by doing that, we are building the groundwork for the collaboration needed in today's work world. Culturally responsive pedagogy, like the Common Core standards, includes teaching students to use critical thinking to investigate their own cultures and the cultures of others by connecting to and engaging with the diversity in our classrooms as well as in the larger world. It also norms diversity, making it okay to be culturally different. In fact, it celebrates differences instead of only searching for similarities. Culturally responsive pedagogy uses technology to power lessons and connect learners to others in lands that are geographically distant, but only seconds apart, to prepare learners to become global citizens. Culturally responsive pedagogy demands we connect the content of our lessons to students' lives, so we must understand the lives our students truly live. This leads to intense self-reflection and investigation of our own prejudices and biases. Using culturally responsive instruction to implement the Common Core breaks down barriers and supports a classroom community poised for learning.

Cultural literacy is awareness of one's own culture and others' cultures coupled with the skills to communicate and interact respectfully with those from cultures that differ from our own. This does not mean that every educator must know and understand every existing culture—an impossible feat, for sure—but it does mean that, as educators, we must understand our own culture. If we are white, for example, we must understand what it means to be part of the dominant culture. We must also strive to know and understand the cultures of the students we teach, yet know that we may never wholly understand. As a result, we must be comfortable knowing that there is much we "don't know we don't know," and we must be open to continue learning. We must be willing to admit to our students that we don't know, and admitting to this unknowing is one of the most challenging aspects of becoming culturally literate.

Becoming Culturally Literate: The Six Steps

Cultural literacy, in many ways, shares attributes with *global literacy* as defined by Vivien Stewart (2010). She writes that global literacy includes the following elements:

- Knowledge of other world regions, culture, economies, and global issues
- Skills to communicate in languages other than English, to work in cross-cultural teams, and to assess information from different sources around the world
- Values of respect for other cultures and the disposition to engage responsibility as an actor in the global context (p. 103)

Cultural literacy begins with the understanding of one's own culture as the starting point for gaining knowledge and respect for other cultures. To become culturally literate, we must take a cultural literacy journey. Cultural literacy is not something you master; rather, it is something you continue to practice in order to improve. The journey begins with communication. Educators committed to cultural literacy must decide the best strategies to use for communicating among staff members.

The journey encompasses a six-step framework for building literacy for the Common Core. This framework is a tool to use during the implementation of standards-based instruction and as you are planning and delivering instruction, reflecting on your interactions with students and colleagues, knowing your impact, and monitoring your personal progress as you continue to grow in cultural literacy. The six steps are described in figure I.1.

Step 1: Build Teacher-Student Relationships by Honoring Visibility and Voice

Teachers acknowledge, validate, and honor each learner. They norm difference and create visibility to engage each individual learner and create a community of learners. They also honor their own voices and those of colleagues.

Step 2: Work and Plan Together Through Collaborative Conversations

Teachers work in professional learning groups using collaborative conversations to plan standards-based instruction using a lens of cultural literacy. They engage in professional walkthroughs in collaborative teams.

Step 3: Use High-Yield, Research-Based Strategies

Teachers use high-yield, research-based strategies as they deliver instruction.

Step 4: Teach Standards-Based Lessons

Teachers deliver high-quality, standards-based instruction using authentic assignments and differentiated instruction.

Step 5: Use Feedback to Self-Assess Learning

Teachers use formative assessment and student feedback to monitor and adjust instruction to ensure that all learners master the standards and use self-reflection to assess instruction and professional growth.

Step 6: Engage in a Cultural Literacy Journey

Staff members work in collaborative conversation groups to continue their journey to learn what they "don't know they don't know" about themselves and others.

Figure I.1: The six-step framework for building cultural literacy for the Common Core.

The Research Behind the Six-Step Framework

The six-step framework is powerful, practical, informal, and interactive; it is intended to be a guide tied directly to the Common Core State Standards that you use to improve your instruction, embed culturally responsive instruction, build better relationships with your students, and achieve better results in student learning. It relies heavily on the research of John Hattie (2009, 2012) and Robert Marzano, Debra Pickering, and Jane Pollock (2001). Research feeds practice, and in this book, we share what works in classrooms based on the research and the experiences of real-world educators. First, the framework is built on sound communication.

Sound Communication

In *Unmistakable Impact: A Partnership Approach for Dramatically Improving Instruction*, Jim Knight (2013) suggests the following communication strategies: "Listen, ask good questions, find common ground, control difficult emotions, and love your partners" (p. 236). Even though Knight's suggestion to find common ground is a good one, at times, we may be on *uncommon ground*, such as when discussing issues of culture or race. Admitting, accepting, and embracing difference and our uncommon ground can be powerful for educators. Working through a process to uncover our differences can allow us to understand what is at the root of our emotions and how we might best learn from and love our colleagues and work together to support the needs of educators and students of color.* Knight's suggestions speak to what we need to do for our colleagues and our students—love them as human beings first, in order to do hard work with them and obtain the best outcomes for them.

In addition to Knight's communication strategies, the four agreements of courageous conversation found in *Courageous Conversations About Race* by Glenn Singleton and Curtis Linton (2006) help educators through the six-step framework: "Experience discomfort, speak your truth, stay engaged, and expect and accept nonclosure" (p. 17).

These four agreements offer a protocol for the cultural literacy journey. Realizing we will not solve the issue of inequity or racism that has permeated our society for centuries allows us to focus on the immediate and personal rather than on what we cannot control. Singleton and Linton's suggestions to experience discomfort and accept nonclosure communicate that the journey will not be easy and will not end; however, it will be rewarding, as evidenced throughout this book in the stories of

---

* Throughout the book, the term *of color* is used to designate a variety of groups, including people of color, communities of color, students of color, and others. I use this term because it is inclusive of all individuals in nonwhite groups. In addition, I use *of color* rather than the term *minority* because *minority* may imply inferiority, and it carries a numerical connotation that no longer works since, in some states, students of color are not the minority in number in our schools.

teachers and staffs that journeyed through discomfort and nonclosure to find a place where they could work and prosper.

These four agreements, in conjunction with Knight's strategies for communication, set the foundation for good communication—a foundation that rests on the ability to communicate assertively rather than resorting to passive or aggressive modes of communication. This is not an easy task for those whose voices have been silenced and who have been socialized to defer to the more powerful voices of others. Within these pages are the stories of educators who are learning to communicate assertively and honor, validate, and make audible the voices of all individuals, both adults and students, in their schools to build a classroom climate in which they can implement the CCSS and increase rigor because they have built a foundation of openness and trust.

Essential Questions

Next, the framework borrows from the work of Grant Wiggins and Jay McTighe (1998, as cited in Singleton & Linton, 2006). In *Courageous Conversations About Race: A Field Guide for Achieving Equity in Schools*, Singleton and Linton expand upon the original three questions posed by Wiggins and McTighe, offering us a vehicle to begin examining ourselves and what we don't know we don't know. They frame these questions in terms of the personal and professional inquiry and action educators must consider as they address the racial achievement gap.

1. What is it that educators should know and be able to do to narrow the racial achievement gap?
2. How will educators know when they are experiencing success in their efforts to narrow the racial achievement gap?
3. What do they do as they discover what they don't yet know and are not yet able to do to eliminate the racial achievement gap? (2006, p. 3)

Additional essential questions include the big ideas that govern our work, such as the following:

*   Why do human beings create hierarchies of power?
*   Why are we afraid of the "other" or "otherness"?
*   Why is darkness given a negative connotation in Western symbolism?
*   Why can't we all just get along (Rodney King's words [CNN Wire Staff, 2012])?
*   What causes people to bond together?
*   How can learning about others or "walking in their shoes" reduce isolation?
*   In what ways can teachers build relationships with all learners, no matter their racial, ethnic, cultural, gender, or religious background?

Good teaching involves examining the big picture and asking the essential questions. The CCSS give us a rigorous framework of instructional standards; the six-step framework gives us a guide for good teaching practice. But what is good teaching?

Good Teaching Practice

Good teaching focuses on the learning rather than on the teaching. As we discussed earlier, Hattie's (2012) findings support the idea that students learn the most when teachers become students of their own learning and learners become their own teachers. *Cultural Literacy for the Common Core: Six Steps to Powerful, Practical Instruction for All Learners* provides many examples of teachers being learners of their teaching; in fact, this is the central idea of the book. When teachers practice deep reflection in interrogating reality, they face the world as learners and continue to grow in awareness and practice.

This cannot be done in isolation. Such knowledge is not new, but there are still too many schools in which teachers teach behind closed doors and do not share their journeys of learning with others (DuFour, DuFour, Eaker, & Many, 2006). The six-step framework presents numerous options for eradicating the isolation of teaching and for increasing effectiveness by working with colleagues as you implement the Common Core. This does not have to be difficult. For example, many years ago, a group of high school teachers decided to meet each Friday morning before school for coffee and twenty minutes of talk time. Because the time was so short (they met from 7:40 to 8:00, when classes began), they focused their conversation by choosing a topic for each week. These topics ranged from student tardiness to homework to classroom management to absenteeism, and others—all important topics to high school teachers. Over the course of the semester, they met about fifteen times, bringing their best ideas to the group. During these sessions, they were able to work together to solve some challenges that detracted from instructional time. One teacher even surveyed his students and asked them what they liked and didn't like about him and the class. He wrote a list of their responses and posted it over his coat hook in his classroom. He began his day by reading the list and determining that he would refrain from the behaviors students didn't like and, instead, focus on what the students liked about him and his instruction. Using their feedback signaled to students that they were respected and that the exercise was worthwhile (Davis, 2007).

Today, many staffs have progressed from sharing procedural ideas (still very important) to examining student work and collecting data on what works and what doesn't work in their instruction as they implement the CCSS. Instruction begins with planning—well before the execution of the lesson. Hattie (2012) writes that when good teaching occurs, there is "an emphasis on planning, being clear about the purposes and outcomes of lessons (both by the teachers and the students), having expectations or targets of what the impact should be, and then continually evaluating the impact of the teacher on the learner" (Kindle location 924). The six-step framework supports this. When teams of teachers work together and are "students of their own impact," learning improves—both for the student and for the teacher and learners reach targets and master standards.

Hattie (2012) defines *excellent teachers* as those who "maintain a passionate belief that students can learn the content and understandings included in the learning intentions of the lesson(s)" (Kindle location 711). *Cultural Literacy for the Common Core* strongly supports this definition. If you strive to be an excellent teacher, you get more of what you focus on, as Becky Bailey (2006) writes, and the six-step framework offers you positive, powerful ways to enhance your instruction and improve the learning of your students. But what does positive, powerful instruction look like in the classroom?

Positive, Powerful Instruction

The strategies presented in this book, for the most part, work across communities of color, and the framework is designed to work with all learners. The framework builds upon and expands earlier models, such as those designed by Madeline Hunter (1982), Knight (2012), Marzano (2012), and Pollock (2012), with two important pieces: teacher-student relationships that emphasize giving visibility and voice to learners and a cultural literacy journey taken with colleagues in collaborative conversations. The framework supports teachers in understanding the need to build relationships by incorporating student visibility and voice into instruction as well as in understanding the need to continue a cultural literacy journey to understand what we don't know we don't know.

How to Use This Book

Throughout the coming chapters, you will find stories from my experience as well as many others from teachers who knew something was missing in their classrooms but did not know what—teachers who became aware enough to realize there were things they didn't know they didn't know. The six-step framework offers educators and others a guide to find their areas of need and ways to strengthen their relationships with and instruction for all learners. The framework functions in several ways:

- To guide your lesson planning and instructional delivery
- To help you self-assess your cultural literacy
- To aid in your efforts to gain strategies and lesson ideas for the classroom

The framework is a structure to support your thinking. In no way is the framework or this book intended to replace a district's professional development for the implementation of the CCSS; rather, the framework and the book are intended to supplement the work already being done and support what needs to occur to infuse cultural literacy into implementation of the CCSS.

This book is set up as six steps of a journey, with one chapter for each step. Each step of the framework is described within one chapter and includes connections to the CCSS as well as real examples from teachers teaching in today's classrooms. As a teacher myself, I believe in sharing real work done in real classrooms. I have been fortunate to work with many teachers, both new and veteran, who want to share their experiences and their lessons—and have done so in this book.

You can work through the book, going from step 1 to step 6, or you can choose a step that most interests you or your group and begin there. Each chapter stands alone, even though all six create a framework for a journey of cultural literacy within the climate of the CCSS. Use this book with your professional learning group or team. Through collaborative conversations, the steps will help you reflect, discuss, and work together to implement standards-based instruction and build your cultural literacy. The steps will help you plan your instruction, evaluate your impact on the learner, and, most of all, learn more about yourself and build better relationships with colleagues and learners in your classroom. This book was designed to enrich your teaching experience. The chapter content is as follows.

Chapter 1: Build Teacher-Student Relationships by Honoring Visibility and Voice

Chapter 1 provides an overview of the research that supports the necessity of building teacher-student relationships. Making the connections can be done in many ways; the chapter emphasizes giving visibility to all students and creating a space where all students' voices are heard, listened to, and valued. This is the first step to implementing the CCSS in your instruction. By beginning with building teacher-student relationships, you create a foundation for academic work.

Chapter 2: Work and Plan Together Through Collaborative Conversations

Today's learners deserve well-planned lessons that bring together myriad resources. In this chapter, I provide examples of how teachers use collaborative conversations to plan together to engage learners and support their learning, including working with literacy coaches and doing classroom walkthroughs to learn from each other as you implement the Common Core.

Chapter 3: Use High-Yield, Research-Based Strategies

Some strategies are more effective than others. In this chapter, you will find high-yield, research-based strategies (and a few fun ones) to incorporate into your teaching repertoire along with numerous implementation examples as you implement the Common Core.

Chapter 4: Teach Standards-Based Lessons

Higher level, standards-based lessons motivate and engage learners. In this chapter, teachers in today's classrooms share their lessons that are aligned to the Common Core.

Chapter 5: Use Feedback to Self-Assess Learning

This chapter offers a feedback model based on the work of Jane Pollock (2012) and supported by Hattie (2012) and Marzano's (2001, 2007, 2009, 2012, 2013) research. In the chapter, Pollock uses feedback to self-assess learning. Teachers share their successes with the model and with additional means of feedback. In addition, teachers reflect on their standards-based practice using data from student surveys.

Chapter 6: Engage in a Cultural Literacy Journey

Working in schools implementing the Common Core, the educators featured in this chapter know they can't lose sight of the challenges facing them, and addressing the increasing diversity of their student body is one such challenge. This chapter outlines the journeys of educators in several districts as they venture into unknown territory and learn what they don't know they don't know about others' cultures and their own. Included are multiple strategies and pathways you can use to take a similar journey.

Beginning Your Journey

Ultimately, this book is about honoring human beings, no matter who they are. It is about the necessity to build relationships in the classroom before we teach the content and continuing to build relationships throughout the teaching of the content. It is about empowering teachers to be able to make decisions about what and when to teach and about empowering learners to join with teachers to question the world and learn together in collaborative inquiry with common curiosity. It is about norming difference and accepting other cultures—in fact, it is about celebrating difference and adjusting our instruction to include cultural practices positively reinforced by other cultures. It is about learning what we don't know we don't know and being willing to examine our impact on each student in our classrooms. It is about the future and learning how to create a better one for all children, growing a more equitable society, and loving those with whom we presently share a learning space. It is about the present and the only time we truly have to make a difference. It is about what you can do now.

CHAPTER 1

Build Teacher-Student Relationships by Honoring Visibility and Voice

Making student voice part of the culture of the school encourages students to invest in their learning and in the broader school community.

—Yvette Jackson

Hattie (2009), in his book *Visible Learning: A Synthesis of Over 800 Meta-Analyses Relating to Achievement*, finds that the teacher-student relationship is one of the top twelve influences on achievement out of 150 influences. Is this surprising to you? We hear so much about teacher-student relationships that the topic seems almost cliché. In fact, when some educators voice the opinion that "it's all about the relationships," other educators sigh and beg for concrete instructional strategies to improve achievement and meet standards. But building relationships *is* a strategy. In fact, it is one of the most powerful strategies we can use to influence student achievement.

Why do you think that building teacher-student relationships is often *not* considered a concrete strategy even though we have research that proves it influences achievement?

Step 1 of the six-step framework asks us to build teacher-student relationships through honoring visibility and voice. Do you believe our relationships with others create expectations for them and influence achievement?

Expectations

According to Marzano (2007), the effect of teacher expectations on student achievement might be one of the most researched areas of classroom instruction. Marzano (2007) states that "a teacher's beliefs about students' chances of success in school influence the teacher's actions with students, which in turn influence students' achievement" (p. 162). Citing Jere Brophy's (1983) synthesis on the research, Marzano (2007) describes teacher behaviors in the affective tone, which differs according to their beliefs about students' abilities. The *affective tone*, or feeling tone of the classroom, refers to behaviors teachers use to establish positive emotions in the classroom. With low-achieving students, teachers take these steps:

- Praise less frequently than with high-achieving students
- Maintain less proximity and less physical contact
- Smile less
- Use friendly nonverbal behaviors less, including playful or light dialogue
- Give less eye contact and nonverbal communication of attention and responsiveness. (as quoted in Marzano, 2007, pp. 166–167)

How do these teacher behaviors impact student academic expectations? Tracey, an African American administrator, shares her experience as a student:

> I think at times African American or other minority students feel inadvertently left out of the academic setting; therefore, their academic performance suffers. As a minority student, I thought some of my teachers just did not like me or care about my academic success. In the classroom, those teachers rarely came in close proximity to me or gave me eye contact. I didn't get asked questions about how I learn best or what my thoughts were. I think it is absolutely necessary to remember that all students need to feel valued and affirmed. If the educator doesn't make it a priority to even be near a minority student when he or she is educating students, it sends the message that the student's learning is not important. (T. Black, personal communication, March 1, 2013)

Clearly, Tracey felt invisible in many of her educational settings. She felt some teachers did not like her or have expectations for her academic success—the teacher-student relationship was lacking.

> *In what ways do you think teacher-student relationships are necessary in the learning process?*

In addition to establishing the affective tone of the classroom through their behaviors and through building relationships with learners, teachers also express their academic expectations of students through the quality of their interactions with learners with high- and low-perceived success. Again citing Brophy's (1983) research synthesis, Marzano (2007) writes that teachers do the following with students perceived as low-achieving:

- Give less wait time and less challenging questions
- Delve less into answers given by these students
- Give less feedback to these students
- Pay less attention to them and interact with them less
- Reward them for less-rigorous responses (Brophy, 1983, as quoted in Marzano, 2007, pp. 166–169)

Think of your own child, a grandchild, or a child you are close to. What if a teacher were treating him or her with such behaviors? How would you feel?

Knowing the research on expectations, what steps can you take to ensure you hold high expectations for all the learners in your classroom?

How do you believe teacher expectations affect the implementation of the Common Core State Standards?

When students perceived as low performers enter a teacher's classroom, they have many barriers to overcome. The biases of the teacher can be a significant barrier. As an award-winning teacher, I thought I held high expectations for all learners in my classroom and was free of such biases. I discovered otherwise.

Much of my work has focused on culturally diverse learners, African American learners, Latino and Latina learners, English learners (ELs), and students in poverty. However, it took me many years and much soul searching to realize I had lower expectations for students of color due to my socialization in the small, segregated, Southern town where I grew up. I had no professional role models of color. My college experience at the University of Mississippi in the 1960s and '70s further embedded my unconscious stereotypes. I walked a campus where I saw no black people except for the gardeners. I was so inured to the experience that I remember once wondering why the foremen on the job were all white and the workers were all black. But even as an intelligent college student, I could not put that question into the larger framework of racism in the United States. I continued to study white male authors and eventually attained a master's degree in English. It was not until I had my own personal relationship with a black man, whom I married and with whom I had a son, that I even began to question my biases and beliefs. I have come far enough on the lifelong journey to understand that my unconscious biases affect my interactions with people of color. I must work vigilantly to avoid unconscious acts of discrimination. Using a standards-based curriculum is one step toward avoiding unconscious acts of discrimination. When we use the Common Core State Standards to guide instruction, we hold each individual learner accountable for reaching the standard. We do not just expect certain kinds of students to be able to master content.

Knowing my own biases, I feared my son's teachers also might hold lower expectations of him, so I monitored them to ensure they held high expectations. Yet, I still found times when I doubted their expectations. Why did the teacher of gifted students express surprise when she learned that my biracial son scored high enough to be placed in a gifted program? Was it because he was black? Did that expectation impact her instruction of him? Was the reason he didn't like the gifted program because of her expectations? My personal experiences have caused me to constantly examine my own responses, biases, and actions.

A simple way to examine your own responses is to use a chart and self-reflect, or ask your school instructional coach (or a colleague if you have no coach) to observe and chart your actions in the classroom. Figure 1.1 provides an example of such a chart. Fill in the chart with the names of students for whom you think you might hold low expectations; then chart your affective and interactive behaviors with each student over several days, or ask your partner or colleague to chart your behaviors.

By using the form in figure 1.1, or something similar, you can see how you are interacting with different students in the class. None of the actions in figure 1.1 are bad, yet the teacher is relating positively to one student, Anthony, in ways that build the relationship. With Melinda, the teacher did not use strategies to build the relationship.

Student	Observed Affective and Interactive Behaviors With Student
Anthony Lopez	Greeted Anthony at the door
	Used proximity to get Anthony back on task
	Asked Anthony if I could help him in any way to get started on the task
	Gave Anthony a choice to either read from his book or continue writing his story
	Called on Anthony two times during class discussion
	Asked Anthony to summarize his learning to the class during the final five minutes of class
	Stood at the door and said goodbye to Anthony as he exited the room
Melinda Miller	Did not see Melinda come into class, so did not have a chance to greet her
	Moved Melinda when she sat next to friends she socializes with too much
	Melinda did not raise her hand during the discussion, so I did not call on her.
	Melinda did not have her homework, and I let her know I was not pleased.
	Melinda left early to see the counselor, so I did not say goodbye at the door.

Figure 1.1: Sample teacher-student interactions chart.

Increasing Visibility

Think about a time when you felt invisible to others. Perhaps you were in a store and the salesperson ignored you and waited on others who arrived after you. Perhaps it was at a party when you felt invisible because you knew no one, and no one was making the effort to come and talk with you. Or, perhaps you were an older teacher in a workshop filled with young, new teachers who seemed in sync with the administrator and your ideas were ignored—or you were the new teacher, and the older teachers looked right past you and ignored your ideas. For some, these experiences may inspire anger and action. For others, they may inspire retreat and inaction.

> *How did these experiences make you feel?*
>
> *How do you respond to feelings of being invisible?*

As teachers, we can support students and help them feel visible by being culturally responsive to their personhood and offering them the validation they deserve. Visibility is the first step in the framework for creating a culturally literate, standards-based classroom, because until one feels visible—validated, acknowledged, accepted—one seldom works at the highest levels of one's potential. At the same time, strategies for increasing visibility must not take away from precious instructional time; therefore, the framework suggests an initial welcoming strategy for visibility followed by additional strategies that are designed to be part of the flow of instruction. This is easier than you might think. In fact, you are probably already using many of these strategies.

> *Think about the strategies you use to make all students visible in your classroom. Write them down, and reflect on how you use them in class.*

Resource Selection

I was fortunate to learn from many committed teachers who happened to be Catholic nuns. They believed in building relationships with students. These women validated me and made me feel visible and part of the classroom community on a daily basis.

Sister Francesca, my high school English teacher, noticed my love of poetry, and not long after we began a poetry unit, she called me aside one morning and handed me a book of Robert Frost's poems. I still have that book today, and it sits on my bookshelf (with its thirty-five cents sticker on it), reminding me that I was visible to my teachers. In fact, Sister Francesca differentiated instruction in the 1960s, although it wasn't called that. She met her students where we were by learning the individual needs and loves of each one of us, and she responded with choices and lessons designed to meet our needs.

I became a high school English teacher because of Sister Francesca. She related literature to our lives and our lives to the writings we read. There was never a separation between her instruction and our experiences, because she made us feel the poetry, the stories, the essays. In fact, she practiced what Dean Bakopoulos (2013) suggests in his essay "Straight Through the Heart" when he writes:

> But how can you teach someone to master language or read literature until he's fallen in love with it? . . . After reading masterworks and feeling the effects a writer can have on their own souls, they want to get out their laptops and try doing the same thing. (p. 27)

This is what Sister Francesca did—she found great literature that touched our souls. When we care enough about our students to touch their spirits as she did, to make students visible in the subject matter we teach, we forge connections—those teacher-student relationships that solidly support academic engagement. In chapter 3 (page 57), you will find examples of lessons designed by teachers to offer students visibility and support student engagement.

Welcoming Behavior

For three and a half years, I taught writing in a men's prison where each week the men filed into a glass-walled room to take my class, and a guard stood outside. As they entered the room, I greeted each man with a welcome and a smile. On the first night of class, I walked down the aisles and shook each man's hand, looked him in the eyes, and said, "Hello." I told each man I expected him to do well in the class. My body language demonstrated I was confident and professional (even though I admit to being nervous when I first turned my back to write on the board). In seven semesters, no man was ever disrespectful to me. After hearing how they had run off former teachers, I attributed my success to the fact that I honored each man as an individual and made certain he was visible in the class each week in the following ways:

- By giving a personal greeting
- By using engaging and rigorous work
- By giving individual feedback
- By expecting participation in class discussions and that the work be completed
- By saying a personal goodbye at the end of class

At the end of class one night, I found a note on my desk. It said, "Thank you for smiling at me. You are the first person who has smiled at me in the seven months I've been here."

Through my teaching experience at the prison, I learned that I needed to meet and greet each learner in the classroom and invite him or her to engage in the learning.

Making others visible so they understand we see them is a lovely compliment, as well as the basis for human respect. During the time I taught at the prison, we created a literary magazine and offered a place for each man to make his thoughts visible in his writings, which were published for others to read. Offering the men the opportunity for their voices to be heard fostered teacher-student relationships and engaged them as learners.

In the K–12 classroom, validating, acknowledging, and making others visible works as a deterrent to misbehavior. When we feel validated, we feel less of a need to act out in order to be noticed. Learners who feel invisible often choose to act out or shut down. Building relationships with learners and making each visible every day is not an option, but a necessity to honor and validate each human being in the room.

One way to build relationships and visibility is to display pictures and self-portraits of students and families in the classroom. In one classroom, the four- and five-year-old students I was observing were so excited to show me the 3 × 5–inch pictures of their families that were on display around the classroom that their teacher had to redirect them. Teachers at North Glendale Elementary display self-portraits students create during the first days of class. This activity offers teachers the opportunity to learn more about how the students perceive themselves. In most classrooms, they are displayed high on the walls and form a beautiful ring of diverse smiling faces that surrounds the learners throughout the day. The myriad of skin colors celebrate the diversity in the room. Figure 1.2 shows a sample of student self-portraits.

Figure 1.2: Student self-portraits on display in the classroom.

Check-In Procedures

It is necessary to begin each day and each learning period with a personal validation for each learner to build teacher-student and student-student relationships. The popular check-in procedure (see figure 1.3, pages 22–23) is still the best way I know to do this. Many teachers have shared how this procedure has transformed their classes when used consistently and when their learners understood the reasons for its use. Using this strategy means teaching the reasoning behind it (and perhaps continuing to reteach it). It has the power to build classroom community in a significant way in less than two minutes a day. Jessica Jones, a secondary teacher in a diverse urban high school, shares that the check-in procedure allows her to build the classroom community she needs in weeks rather than the months it used to take her before she began using the strategy (J. Jones, personal communication, October 2011).

The check-in procedure presented in figure 1.3 is an opening ritual that transitions into the instructional period. It allows for laughter, bonding, visibility, and validation. You can adapt it to fit your learners. It works in a classroom for several reasons including the following.

- It honors every voice and allows every voice to be heard in a positive manner.
- There is no wrong answer.
- It transitions the brain from outside the classroom.
- It cues the brain it's time to focus.
- It gives feedback about the students to the teacher.
- It builds community.
- It provides peers with knowledge of other peers.
- It allows for humor.
- It can link the activity to the content to be taught—or not.
- It is an ice-breaker.
- It reduces stress and threat.
- It offers novelty in the answers each day.
- It offers routine and ritual, and the brain craves both novelty and ritual.

You can use the check-in procedure at the beginning of class (the most common use), during class for a brain break, to connect to content, or at the end of class to fill time or for feedback on the content students learned. Use a question from the list, or ask students to suggest a question.

Directions for the check-in:

1. Describe the check-in to students, and tell them why you are doing it.

2. Tell students you are going to ask them a question. They must answer the question with one word or one phrase. Demonstrate what a phrase is if they do not know.

3. Tell them they must use a voice loud enough to be heard throughout the classroom.

4. Tell them they may repeat an answer another student says.

5. If they choose not to answer, they may say, "Pass." Spell out *pass* for them.

6. Tell students they may not use profanity or give an inappropriate answer.

7. Demonstrate the process, and ask students why they think you are doing the check-in. (By articulating the reasoning in their own words, they are demonstrating their understanding of what you said.)

8. Check for understanding by role-playing a couple of times.

Possible questions for the check-in:

- What is your favorite _____? (Number, color, TV show, season of the year, school class, day of the week, time of day, food, movie, book, music, fast food restaurant, and so on)

- What sport or school activity do you participate in?

- Where is one place you have traveled?

- What profession are you most interested in pursuing?

- How many siblings do you have?

- What month is your birthday in?

- Are you a cat or dog person?

- What is your favorite mathematical shape?

- How many hours did you play video games yesterday?

- How well did you understand yesterday's lesson on a scale of one to ten?

- How many texts did you send yesterday?

- How long did it take you to get to school?

- What chores do you do at home?

- Can you boil an egg?

- How did you get to school?

- What language other than English can you speak? Name one of them.

- Where were you born?

- What year were you born?

- What was most difficult question on last night's homework?

- What elective would you like to see at this school?
- Where would you like to go on vacation?
- Do you dream in color?
- Have you ever ridden a horse?
- Have you milked a cow?
- What is the scariest amusement park ride you have ridden?
- Can you stand on your head?
- What is your favorite time of day or night?

Figure 1.3: Check-in procedure and sample questions.

Discovering Student Interests

When you discover your students' interests, you possess a key to making students visible. Learn just one interest, and you can ask questions, make conversations, and engage the student when he or she enters the classroom or during the final minutes of class. Most student interests fall into categories, so it is not too difficult to remember them. For example, most adolescents enjoy music, so as a teacher of adolescents, you can ask your students what music they enjoy. Then play music, including student favorites, as students enter the classroom as well as during selected activities. This strategy is a less public one. It can be something special between you and the student. You may both share a love for a certain poet, television show, craft, video game, or sport, for example.

Within Instruction

Visibility within instruction allows for visibility in a more sustained way, such as within the *do now*—the work posted on the board for the learners to do after they enter the room. For example, in a secondary English classroom, the do now might be a journal prompt that ties to the lesson for the day. For example, if students are beginning to read *The House on Mango Street*, the prompt might ask them to write a few sentences about how they received their name—since the first chapter of the book focuses on names. If there are any English learners whose first language is Spanish, consider having a copy of this text in Spanish and asking these learners if they would like to read the section in Spanish. You are honoring the language of these learners by doing this.

Following the journaling, the teacher might ask students to share what they wrote in small groups and then choose one person from each group to share with the entire class. This type of activity works with content knowledge as well. For example, if the teacher is doing a review of direct instruction on prepositions that she taught during a minilesson the previous day, she may ask her students to write a paragraph with as many prepositional phrases as they can accommodate. Following that, students can share their paragraphs with a partner and read them aloud. Then, they can read the same paragraph, eliminating all of the prepositional phrases. They can follow that with an exercise (developed by Mary Kim Schreck*, 2013), during which students circle all the prepositions they find in quotes taken from *The Hunger Games*. Or, consider initiating a "banned pronoun day" as a way to teach students what a pronoun is in the context of their speaking and writing. In this activity, students eliminate the banned pronoun from their writing and speaking for the day and both teachers and students point out when others use a banned pronoun—all in the spirit of fun.

When teachers use sharing, reading, and talking exercises such as these, they offer students numerous opportunities within each class period to be visible to their classmates, to connect with others, to strengthen their own learning, to strengthen the learning community, and to make learning fun.

At the End of the Lesson

The *final five* is using the final five minutes of class (perhaps on Fridays only) for students to share what is on their minds. This is a way to make students visible and also to check in on what might be weighing on them. The final five minutes can richly build the learning community, and it can also be used as a reward for time on task for the previous hour.

All of these examples offer ways for teachers to embed cultural literacy within the instruction without taking away too much instructional time. These practices support a classroom environment that makes each student feel visible and validated, while at the same time building the teacher-student relationship and the relationship among classmates. The following are additional strategies for making learners visible in the classroom.

- Post pictures and posters that reflect the diversity in your classroom, as well as images of people from other cultures, including images of authors, researchers, scientists, historical figures, and characters from books.

---

* Mary Kim, author of *You've Got to Reach Them to Teach Them* (2011) and *From Tired to Inspired* (2013), taught for thirty-six years in secondary schools. Today, she is my colleague, confidant, and co-creator. As we read the research and everything else we can get our hands on, we continue our conversation, usually via email, text, phone, and Facebook, about our own past instruction and student learning.

- Give surveys to students throughout the year to learn at least one interest of each of your students. Use this when you communicate with learners.
- Embed the pair-share strategy into your lessons so that learners have face-to-face communication with other students during each lesson.

Decreasing Invisibility

When we practice cultural literacy, we make learners visible, listen to their voices, and honor and validate them. But do some learners present more of a challenge than others?

What learners present the greatest challenge to you?

For white teachers, do students of color present more of a challenge because they do not look like us? This may not be the case in your experience, but there is evidence that some educators perceive students of color as the "other." Pedro Noguera (2008) writes about the phenomenon of black boys as being perceived as the other. He says that "black males in American society are in trouble" (p. xi). He states, "Although they comprise a relatively small portion of the American population (less than 6 percent), black males occupy a large space within the American psyche and imagination. Throughout much of American history, black males have served as the ultimate 'other'" (p. xi). In this case, *other* means one who is not ourselves—who is different, and the state of otherness is a noun defined as the quality or state of being other or different.

Are the black males in your school academically achieving at the same levels as the rest of your learners?

If they aren't, what do you believe are the reasons?

If black boys have served as the ultimate other, what does that mean in the context of our classroom? How do we make them visible in positive ways so their positive visibility is the norm? What do we do to ensure they do not assume the position of the other through a negative hypervisibility? If they are visible, is it through negative attention? Think about football players for a moment. Football players are especially visible when they make a touchdown. Some black football players began doing movements in the end zone after a touchdown, and their actions went from interesting to not allowed. Why were their movements frowned upon? Would their actions—their hypervisibility—have received as much attention had the players been white?

Noguera (2008) writes that the very presence of black males, "particularly when they are encountered in groups, has been regarded as a menace to innocents (particularly white women) and a potential danger to the social order" (p. xi). Their existence as a problem has been so pervasive in our society that it has become normalized. What does it mean when something has become normalized? To become *normalized* means that something occurs so regularly in our thinking that we do not see it as abnormal. Think about stories of crime on the evening news; are the perpetrators mostly men and women of color? Is this what we expect? What about in the room in your school in which in-school suspension is held? Is it filled with students of color? What about the advanced placement classes? Are they filled with Asian and white students? Does your staff expect the achievement gap in your school to be between whites and African Americans? Does your staff ever talk about the achievement gap between Asian students and white students? These are all examples of our normalized expectations, and we need to think deeply about how we may normalize negativity toward black males. Does the normalization of negativity regarding black males include a subconscious fear of these learners? If I possess a subconscious fear of black males, how can my unconscious body language during my instruction be anything other than negative?

> *Reflect on your body language. How do you think you respond when you are around males of color?*

Black boys—and of course, all students of color—deserve their voices to be heard and their visibility to be positive. Why do we focus on black males? We focus on black males because, if they are doing well academically, others most likely are as well. If your school does not have black males, then focus on the males of color in the school. How well are the Latino learners succeeding in your school?

> *What things in your school setting can you and your colleagues do to ensure your males of color are visible?*

Recall the earlier words from Tracey, who felt ignored and overlooked in the classroom and that her voice did not matter. When we don't believe our voice is heard, we often disconnect from the learning. Initiating a lesson without honoring and respecting every voice in the classroom is a setup for instruction to fail. Instruction should begin with acknowledgment in some concrete, overt way. When a person is overtly acknowledged, he or she becomes a visible part of the classroom community.

This builds teacher-student relationships. In writing about students of color, author Geneva Gay (2000) says that culturally responsive pedagogy teaches students:

> How to apply new knowledge generated by various ethnic scholars to their analyses of social histories, issues, problems, and experiences. These learning engagements encourage and enable students to find their own voices, to contextualize issues in multiple cultural perspectives, to engage in more ways of knowing and thinking, and to become more active participants in shaping their own learning. (p. 35)

In *The Will to Lead, the Skill to Teach: Transforming Schools at Every Level*, authors Sharroky Hollie and Anthony Muhammad (2012) suggest teachers practice culturally and linguistically responsive (CLR) teaching and learning to validate and affirm the "home cultural and linguistic behaviors of the students through selected instructional practices for the purposes of building and bridging the student to increased success in the cultural and linguistic demands of academia (school) and mainstream society" (p. 79). This definition is focused on culture, language, teaching, and learning and is not one size fits all; instead, it is differentiated instruction based on transforming the instructional dynamic for the teacher as well as the student around cultural and linguistic differences. This kind of culturally responsive pedagogy firmly supports the Common Core State Standards by calling for engaging in more ways of knowing and thinking, and for students to be more active participants in their own learning, and in this case, with a basis in their own indigenous culture. These kinds of learning engagements encourage and enable students to find their own voices, Gay (2000) asserts, and note that when we have a voice, we feel heard. Coming to understand another culture can be challenging for teachers, but it is a necessity to reach and teach all learners and to believe that their perceptions are important parts of their learning. Hattie (2012) says it is "only those teachers who have the mind frame that students' perceptions are important who make the sustained efforts needed to engage students more in learning" (Kindle location 894–897).

The learner's voice is a natural outgrowth of visibility. When learners feel visible, they feel they are being heard. Finding ways to include learners' voices into assignments usually means more engagement, better classroom community, and increased completion of assignments. An added bonus is that it makes learning fun. Yvette Jackson (2011) writes that "amplifying student voice is closely linked to situating learning in the lives of students and building relationships. Making student voice part of the culture of the school encourages students to invest in their learning and in the broader school community" (p. 99). When students feel their voices are heard, they begin to feel like part of the broader school community.

> *How do you include the voices of learners within your lessons?*

The following are some examples of ways to include learners' voices in your classroom. They highlight visibility and voice. Although these lessons address more Common Core State Standards and corresponding college and career readiness anchor standards (CCRA) than are listed, those found in the following sections are examples of some of the standards taught during these lessons.

School Directory

This assignment works best at the beginning of the year, so students can learn about their school. Students collaboratively write a school directory for which they investigate an area of study, interview a teacher, or examine some part of the school experience and then write about it. Learners sign up for their area of study, complete their investigation or interview, write a short report in chapter format, and turn it into the teacher for inclusion in the school directory. After the teacher reviews the chapters and students revise their work, the directories are copied and distributed to learners as a guide to their school year.

This lesson engages the following Common Core standards (NGA & CCSSO, 2010), among others:

W.9–10.2—Write informative/explanatory texts to examine and convey complex ideas, concepts, and information clearly and accurately through the effective selection, organization, and analysis of content. (p. 45)

W.9–10.5—Develop and strengthen writing as needed by planning, revising, editing, rewriting, or trying a new approach, focusing on addressing what is most significant for a specific purpose and audience. (p. 46)

Even though these standards are from the original lesson developed by the teacher, you can find the same standards at your grade level for your learners.

Anchor standards (NGA & CCSSO, 2010):

CCRA.W.2—Write informative/explanatory texts to examine and convey complex ideas and information clearly and accurately through the effective selection, organization, and analysis of content. (p. 18)

CCRA.W.5—Develop and strengthen writing as needed by planning, revising, editing, rewriting, or trying a new approach. (p. 18)

Poetry Books

Students begin by reading many poems in order to identify one that speaks to them. Then they write about it: analyze the poem, another poem related to the first, or a creative piece that addresses or corresponds with the poem in some way. After completing the writing process, learners submit their pieces for inclusion in a class poetry book. This book becomes part of the classroom library that students can access during sustained silent reading time.

This activity addresses the following Common Core standards (NGA & CCSSO, 2010), among others:

> **RL.9-10.10**—By the end of grade 9 [and grade 10], read and comprehend literature, including stories, dramas, and poems in the grades 9-10 text complexity band proficiently, with scaffolding as needed at the high end of the range. (p. 38)

> **L.9-10.5**—Demonstrate understanding of figurative language, word relationships, and nuances in word meanings. (p. 53)

Anchor standards (NGA & CCSSO, 2010):

> **CCRA.R.10**—Read and comprehend complex literary and informational texts independently and proficiently. (p. 35)

> **CCRA.L.5**—Demonstrate understanding of figurative language, word relationships, and nuances in word meanings. (p. 57)

Authentic Issues

In this activity, learners decide on an issue of importance they want to study. For example, one class decided to study the issue of recycling. Students researched their city's policy on recycling and eventually changed it using their voices by writing letters to the city council, offering solutions for recycling in the schools, and volunteering to carry out some of the work themselves. These learners saw their voices truly make a difference and change the way their community functioned.

This activity addresses the following Common Core standards (NGA & CCSSO, 2010), among others:

> **W.9-10.1**—Write arguments to support claims in an analysis of substantive topics or texts, using valid reasoning and relevant and sufficient evidence. (p. 41)

> **RI.9-10.1**—Cite strong and thorough textual evidence to support analysis of what the text says explicitly as well as inferences drawn from the text. (p. 38)

Anchor standards (NGA & CCSSO, 2010):

> **CCRA.W.1**—Write arguments to support claims in an analysis of substantive topics or texts, using valid reasoning and relevant and sufficient evidence. (p. 42)
>
> **CCRA.R.1**—Read closely to determine what the text says explicitly and to make logical inferences from it; cite specific textual evidence when writing or speaking to support conclusions drawn from the text. (p. 60)

Exit Slips

Exit slips are another way students can express their voices simply and easily. Place the exit slips in a box near the door, and ask students to take one when they enter each day, complete it, and hand it in as they leave. Standing at the door and collecting the exit slips offers another opportunity for you to relate to each learner and give him or her visibility. For example, teachers might use exit slips such as the one in figure 1.4.

Name:
What did you learn today?
What were you supposed to learn today?
What do you like about what we did in class?
What do you wish we had done differently?

Figure 1.4: Sample exit slip.

Before asking students to complete the exit slips, discuss them with students, explaining possible responses. You might explain that the students should have learned the learning target. Some things they may like about class might be learning in groups, the opportunity to work independently on a project, or the reading or writing time. Finally, what they might have wanted to do differently might be to work more in groups or not to work in groups. Giving students a frame for their thoughts allows them to more confidently express their voice.

The next step is up to you. Exit slips provide you with important feedback as you reflect on the success of the day's lesson. Did the learners acknowledge the learning target? If not, is it because they did not meet the target, or does it suggest deeper issues? If students are refusing to respond on their exit slips, does that tell you they are disengaged or unmotivated?

Checkout

The check-out procedure works just as the check-in procedure, except you use it at the end of the class hour, day, or even week. Check-out questions can relate to the content just learned or future content, or they can be just-for-fun questions. Once again, you must teach and reteach the procedure. If students do not participate in check out, consider whether they are engaged during the lesson and, if not, why they are not.

The Teacher Goodbye

When we go to a party, we greet the hosts and are greeted by our hosts; when we leave, we do the same, saying goodbye and thank you. You may not get your learners to say thank you every day when they leave, but you can be the host or hostess who thanks them for their effort and participation. Being warmly urged out the door with a big smile from the teacher lets students enter the hall on a positive note. This is not just for elementary students; older students—and even adults—need this human interaction.

To have a voice and be visible, students need to feel accepted and part of the classroom community. You can ensure this happens by using the strategies suggested in this chapter. These strategies are probably not new to you; yet too often, they are not implemented in classrooms. Are these strategies used in all the classrooms in your school?

Regina Gleason, a middle school teacher at Margaret Buerkle Middle School in Missouri, conducted an action-research project to find out whether her relationship with her students would change when she incorporated positive exchanges (Gleason, 2007, cited in Schreck, 2011). She shares how she built relationships with a majority English learner Bosnian population in her school—adolescents who shared a culture that in many ways differed from Regina's own African American culture.

Every year that I have taught eighth grade, my students and I have gone through a cycle of behavior. At the beginning of the year, I have to be a disciplinarian. Most of my students don't care for me very much because of the discipline I impose in the class environment. I usually don't mind the less-popular status because I am aware of the outcomes. . . . After three months of learning what to expect in my class, they know what to do. By the time the semester changes and during the entire second semester, my students and I have a great time in class. I can laugh and smile a lot easier, and so can they. . . . Unfortunately this year, it did not happen. The transformation of the classroom was totally nonexistent. I was at a complete loss as to why, this year, my students still didn't seem to understand what the expectations were in my class. I continually had to explain simple processes to my students. I seemed to have very little connection with the majority of my students. This is highly unusual.

I decided the best way to increase my connection and relationship with my students was to increase the number of positive exchanges with them. To do this, I decided to keep track of the conversations I had with my students throughout each day.

I chose five students from each class. I selected these students because I was concerned about my interaction with them the most. Some of the students were off task often. Because of their behavior, our communication consisted mostly of my correcting them or explaining to them the negative consequences of their actions. I chose these students so that we would have more positive exchanges to balance the frequent negative conversations. The next kind of student I chose was the student that I didn't know very well. I felt that I needed to talk to them so that they wouldn't slip through the cracks. I wanted to be sure to develop a relationship with my quieter students. I found that, in the past, our interactions were limited because of the attention I had to give to students who were either off task or needed special attention with academics.

I developed a checklist for myself to keep track of the interactions I had with these students each day. On the checklist were each student's name, the day, and a space for the conversation we had. I did include some notes about what the outcomes of some of the conversations had been as well.

The conversations were simple. I usually didn't have much time, so I made sure I greeted or saluted each student. On most occasions I was able to successfully engage them in small exchanges. The short conversations ranged from weather comments to success at school, to the kinds of gum we chewed. I continued to keep track of the conversations I had with each student for three weeks. It was not easy to reach every kid that I had chosen, but I was able to casually engage each student in simple conversations throughout a three-week period.

Eventually, I began to see a change in my classroom. As I began conversations with one of my key students, I was able to talk to others as well. Where one student was available, several students were there as well. I couldn't just talk to one without the others. This happened time and time again. I would approach one of my target students in class or the hall and other students would join in the conversation. They would join in very willingly, in fact. I was very pleased with the contact I had with all of my students.

I found that not only had my students changed, but I changed. My attitude was better. For example, my journal writing inspired a more positive attitude in myself. After reading it, I realized that I really liked my students a lot more than I was conscious of. This new insight made me see past the negative behaviors of my students and focus on the positive.

Since I set the tone for the entire class, the classes became better. I felt good approaching my students. I made them smile with small talk, and they made me smile. I began to look forward to my students and they seemed to feel the same way. During a very short period (three weeks) my students and I felt much better about each other. After a while, the students began to approach me with conversations. Students that I hadn't otherwise had much contact with began to approach me. During passing time, I was in the hall doing hall duty, and I looked out of a nearby window. As I was looking out, one of my chosen students came to the window and stood next to me. He looked out of the window and began to ask about the weather. Even though I had been making conversation with him, this was the first time this student approached me with a conversation.

The students, who were usually off task, did change their behavior. Now, when they are off task, they either correct themselves without my direction, or I only need to give them very little direction for them to focus their attention on their studies. With this group of students, I have more positive exchanges than I have negative, corrective conversations. With all of the students that I chose that had behavior issues, I have definitely seen a change in their behavior. Although some of them do still have issues, most of the students that I chose for the study have very few, if any, behavior problems now.

The quiet students that I didn't have much contact with now approach me more often. I see them in the hall, and they start conversations with me. In one class, I have a student that was diagnosed with depression. . . . He was very quiet, and I rarely spoke with him. I would go days without having contact with him. After I had approached him several times with short conversations, I was out in the hall doing hall duty and as he was approaching the classroom, he exclaimed, "How you doing, Ms. Gleason?" I was so shocked that I gasped before I was able to respond to him.

In the end, my class changed more because I changed. When my attitude changed, then my students' did as well. (Gleason, 2007, as cited in Schreck, 2011, pp. 9–12, reprinted with permission)

After three weeks of focusing on positive exchanges, Regina reported the following results:

- I feel much better as a teacher.
- My good attitude sets the tone in the class, and improves the students' attitudes.
- I see more smiles.
- I give more smiles.
- It's better to be more conscious of your attitude.
- The students and I laugh more.
- My classes run more smoothly.
- I don't have to correct inappropriate behaviors as much.
- As I increased positive interactions with the students I chose to

focus on for the study, my positive interactions with other students
increased as well.

- A small action resulted in a significant positive environmental change
in my classes (as cited in Schreck, 2011, pp. 10–12)

You can perform a similar action-research project to see how positive exchanges
build your relationships with your students. Middle school and high school teachers,
choose one class during your day and do the five steps Regina did for three weeks
straight (fifteen school days):

1. Greet all students at the door as they come into the room.
2. Choose five students to focus on, and develop a checklist to keep track of
   interactions and conversations with them.
3. Hold the conversations with the target students, and increase casual conversations with all students.
4. Track data on the checklist.
5. Reflect on the data, and make changes in instruction for all students.

Pay attention to the differences you observe in the behaviors of your most challenging students. Are you receiving more smiles? Are learners more engaged?

Elementary school teachers typically do the first step—they greet and hug their
students as they enter the classroom. Many use circle time to do a check-in and greet
all the children. Additionally, they line students up and love them out the door, too.
But, ask yourself how much student voice is involved in your lessons. How much
reflection on what has been learned is embedded throughout the day? If you are an
elementary teacher, you may want to focus on student voice and feedback. Perhaps
choose one subject you teach and infuse the instruction for that subject with student
voice and feedback, then compare it to student engagement in other subjects. Do this
for a sustained number of days, and reflect on your findings.

Using Voice as an Observation Tool

No teacher wants to do a bad job. We want to be effective, teach our students, and
have them learn what we teach. In chapter 5, "Use Feedback to Self-Assess Learning"
(page 121), we examine specific feedback during lessons. But right now, let's consider
how student voice can give you feedback about your instructional effectiveness in a
more global way. There are simple ways to elicit feedback or comments from students
that can greatly impact your effectiveness. Who would know better than the students
what works and what doesn't work? The Hanover Research Council (2009) reports

the correlation between student feedback about teacher effectiveness and student achievement.

At the end of a unit or the quarter, ask students questions such as, "What worked for you in this unit?" "What didn't work?" "What might I (the teacher) have done differently or better so that you might have better learned the material in the unit?" Read the responses and decide what you can do to modify your instruction. Make a list of things students like and don't like, and post it in your classroom to remind you throughout the day.

Use a strategy such as pair-share for feedback. Pair-share can be as simple as asking students to turn to a partner and share what they just heard you say or what they saw and heard in a video or online. The next time you use the strategy, ask learners for feedback on how well they like it and how well they think they learn when you use it. Asking students for their input on classroom pedagogy honors learners and tells them you truly expect them to achieve.

Students typically enjoy group work. They enjoy sitting with their peers and interacting with them during lessons. If you are incorporating group work, what is working and what is not working in the groups? Ask your students to use their voices to clue you in. Treat them as experts and learn from them.

In addition to learning from students, we can learn from their families. Teachers who tap into families' voices build alliances and support. Teachers can take several simple actions to support families' voices in their children's educational experiences. Consider the following strategies.

- Call home before school begins, and introduce yourself to the family.
- Say hello to any adults you see on school grounds. Too often staff miss this opportunity to build goodwill.
- Incorporate activities at the beginning of the year that touch parents' and caregivers' hearts. For example, ask students to ask their family members about experiences they want to share. Consider surveys that honor families' traditions and experiences.
- Ask parents or caregivers to write a letter or email describing their child to his or her teacher.
- Send home a parent or caregiver volunteer page to ask for help in the classroom. Family members might do the following:
  - Read to students.
  - Listen to students read and share their writing.

- Take students for one or more *walk and talks*—a walk with students where the adult talks informally with students as they walk the neighborhood or some other designated area.
  - Monitor students using computers.
  - Do math games with students.
  - Play educational computer games with students.
  - Do special art projects with students.
- Hold special events to connect with families. For example, do an oral history project, and invite families to listen to the students read their oral histories to the group. Or, host a writers' showcase for families where students read their creative writing pieces, and each family leaves with a book of class writings.

Conclusion

The strategies in this chapter offer opportunities to give visibility and voice to the learners in your classroom.

What ideas or strategies will you commit to trying?

Next, reflect on the direct link between building teacher-student relationships and teaching a standards-based curriculum using the CCSS.

What links do you find between building teacher-student relationships and teaching a standards-based curriculum?

I hope that after reading this chapter, you agree that building relationships with learners and making each learner visible every day is not an option, but a necessity. It is a necessity for us as teachers if we are to develop cultural literacy and reach and teach all learners. Our 21st century learners may reach first for their technological devices to communicate, but if they do not have a human heart reaching out to them in the classroom, many of them will disengage and join the masses of invisible students who drop out of the educational system each year.

As you work to implement the CCSS and standards-based instruction, do not forget to lead with your heart. Build the relationship first, and the student will be ready to learn. Step 1 offers you a pathway that is loving and kind—and allows each student to know he or she is valued and visible in your eyes.

This step is not something we do alone. In order to support each student in finding the pathway to educational equity, we need the help of others. Those others are our colleagues, and together with them, we can plan and execute educational experiences that offer our students a village of educational opportunity.

The next chapter focuses on working with others in professional learning groups and planning for standards-based instructional lessons that honor and validate each member of the educational community.

CHAPTER 2

Work and Plan Together Through Collaborative Conversations

*Change the world—
one conversation
at a time.*

—Susan Scott

S tep 2 in the framework outlines ways to work together in collaborative conversations to plan and implement lessons and instruction using the CCSS. In this chapter, we expand the concept of cultural literacy to include teachers learning more about what they don't know they don't know as they plan and reflect together. This step supports educators as we change paradigms: we are no longer the individual teacher teaching behind closed doors; instead, in the 21st century, we are members of a collaborative team of lifelong learners who grow through collaboration and collegial conversations. As we work together to implement the CCSS, we need to incorporate more complex texts, nonfiction, and text sets. We need to find ways for more student talk and less teacher talk. We need to collaborate with our colleagues on ways to include more project-based learning. We need to immerse learners in argumentative writing using critical-thinking skills, and we need to move learners from memorization to understanding. Collaborative conversations within professional learning groups are the vehicle for accommodating this paradigm shift and implementing the CCSS.

In your school, do you collaborate through conversations with others in professional learning groups? In what ways do the groups support your learning?

Collaborative groups support learning by providing opportunities for adults within an organization to continue learning with a shared focus on and commitment to student learning (DuFour et al., 2006). Although ultimately focused on student learning, professional learning groups understand that they must begin with themselves. Examining thoughts and behaviors through conversations and collaboration allows teachers to become culturally literate about their own culture and how it impacts their communication with all learners in their school setting.

Hattie (2012) writes that the most successful method he has encountered for planning together and discussing the progression of student learning is a data teams process. In this model, small teams meet every two or three weeks (at a minimum) and use "an explicit, data-driven structure to disaggregate data, analyze student performance, set incremental goals, engage in dialogue around explicit and deliberate instruction, and create a plan to monitor student learning and teacher instruction" (Kindle location 1500). Hattie (2012) describes the following four-step process:

1. Collect and chart the data.
2. Use the evidence to "prioritize and set, review, and revise incremental goals."
3. Question the instructional strategies.
4. Monitor the impact of these strategies and impact on student learning. (Kindle location 1514)

In this new paradigm of collaborative conversations, educators move from viewing the educational landscape from their individual viewpoints as single classroom teachers to understanding that each teacher impacts the achievement of every learner in the building.

In the 1980s, my son went to a small public elementary school called the Webster Groves Elementary Computer School in Rock Hill, Missouri. The Computer School was a K–5 school with twenty-two students per class. There were six teachers at the school—each teacher teaching one grade level. So each teacher had all the school's students in the classroom at some point during the student's tenure. Because of this, each teacher felt ownership for all 132 students, and the teachers truly ran the school according to the dictum, "It takes a village to raise a child." Even though students were placed in the school by lottery and not based on test scores, the school scored in the top five, and sometimes number one, on state tests in math and communication arts. Years later, I interviewed teachers at the school about their success. They remarked that they achieved success because they functioned as one entity for the purpose of educating each student in the school; in other words, they took responsibility for every student and collaborated through their conversations to create excellence.

Michael Fullan (2008) echoes this sense of purpose when he points out that in successful institutions:

> All stakeholders are rallying around a *higher purpose* that has meaning for individuals as well as for the collectivity. . . . *Identifying* with an entity larger than oneself expands the self, with powerful consequences. Enlarged identity and commitment are the social glue that enable large organizations to cohere. (p. 49)

The staff at The Computer School obviously identified with something larger than themselves and their individual classrooms. They planned together and ate together as one big, usually happy family; they were not the typical isolated teachers behind closed doors too often found during the 1980s. Hattie (2012) writes that it is not the teachers who are responsible for all students learning or not learning, but rather it is a "collective, school-wide responsibility to ensure that all students are making at least a year's growth for a year's input, and to work together to diagnose, recommend interventions, and collectively evaluate the impact of teachers and programs" (Kindle location 1569).

Collaboration and conversations are not new in education, but in the past, they may have occurred serendipitously; today they are a necessity. In the 21st century, we need to learn to work together in collaborative teams and use conversations to bring about change. According to Fullan (2008), change involves love, and he advocates that school leaders should "love your employees." I was particularly struck by his use of the word *love*. It is common to reiterate that we need to respect others, but we usually don't find *love* included in suggestions for working with colleagues. But I love that he uses *love*. In fact, Knight (2011) further expands this notion, saying, "If we are going to explore healthy relationships, we simply have to suck it up and talk about love, even love at school" (p. 228). Talking about love for colleagues and students in the school setting changes the dynamics of our conversations. Consider your own feelings.

Do you feel love for your colleagues and students?

Fierce Conversations

One way to begin to engage in a meaningful exchange with love is to hold fierce conversations. Susan Scott (2002), in the book *Fierce Conversations: Achieving Success at Work and in Life, One Conversation at a Time*, defines a *fierce conversation* as "one in which we come out from behind ourselves into the conversation and make it real" (p. 7). By this, Scott means that individuals must "master the courage to interrogate reality" (p. xv). Mastering the courage to interrogate reality is a challenge, and it is an especially difficult one in some schools where the staff works so hard at being nice. In a climate consisting largely of white, middle-class females, often over the age of fifty (and I am one of these women), it is not an easy adjustment to suddenly find the courage to interrogate reality and discuss issues honestly and openly. Consider the following example.

In one elementary school, the staff worked hard to weave social interaction into their days. They had studied the book *Courageous Conversations About Race* (Singleton & Linton, 2006) and incorporated culturally themed luncheons, focusing on such cultures as Mexican, Italian, and others, each month. When a white staff member suggested a soul food luncheon the Friday before Martin Luther King Jr. Day, another faculty member thought the suggestion might be racist. This comment divided the staff—especially because the group had been working on equity. If a staff member is afraid of the words *soul food*, then what other cultural phrases are staff members afraid to confront, interrogate, or use? Were members of this staff ready to have a fierce conversation? Were they ready to come out from behind themselves into the conversation and make it real?

Fortunately, this staff did confront the issue and interrogated it by learning together about soul food. The group researched soul food on the Internet and discussed the findings. The staff shared recipes and cooked soul food dishes for the luncheon. It was a highly successful day. As a result of working together to build a community where members love each other, the staff was able to discuss a difficult issue and work through it. But how did this staff arrive at the point where they could have fierce and courageous conversations? They did it through practice and specific strategies.

One such strategy is a book study. The staff at North Glenridge Elementary School holds a book study of the text *Conscious Discipline: 7 Basic Skills for Brain Smart Classroom Management* by Bailey (2001) before school once a month. The study is voluntary, because before school does not work for all staff members, but the staff who attend find it to be a rich, therapy-like session to begin their day. They follow this schedule.

7:30–7:40 a.m.: Welcome and conversation

7:40 a.m.: Check-in question to honor and make visible every voice and welcome each staff member

7:45 a.m.: Discussion of content from the book in small groups with a lot of sharing, usually covering a few pages each session, and doing the activities listed in the book

8:15 a.m.: Check-out question and response to honor, make visible, and thank each participating member

As the facilitator for this book study, I found the study to be an effective way to support staff in working together collaboratively and interrogating the truth of their classrooms. Because the content of *Conscious Discipline* focuses on inner change, the group members focused on our inner selves and how we relate to and love (or not) our colleagues and our students. Because our group was mostly white females, we deepened our conversations about the hidden rules under which we operate and how they manifest themselves with our colleagues and our students. These hidden rules include behaviors such as our desire to please, our hesitancy to engage in conflict, and our use of indirect language when giving directions, to name a few. Following are some of the participants' comments.

Because teaching encompasses more than academics, which we discuss 90 percent of our time, it's helpful to have a forum in which we can discuss classroom management and taking care of ourselves. It's great getting real with our colleagues. And refreshing! (M. Woodard, fourth-grade teacher, personal communication, March 27, 2013)

I enjoy the time with teachers to reflect on ourselves and how who we are affects what we do. One big "Ah Ha" moment for me this year was when we did our study of empathy and how we deal with students who are acting out. I have always secretly judged people who did not show empathy to students who were struggling—either behaviorally or academically. Now I realize that we treat those situations the way our parents did. If we were raised without empathy, then we will probably not have much empathy when we deal with our students. I see now that it is not right or wrong, it is simply who we are. I appreciate that after this discussion. (J. Belinki, math coach and math specialist, personal communication, March 27, 2013)

Interrogating the truth together is a sometimes-painful endeavor, but it pays off as staff members develop greater empathy for others and, just as importantly, for themselves. The following books have also been the subject of book studies using this format:

- *Daring Greatly: How the Courage to Be Vulnerable Transforms the Way We Live, Love, Parent, and Lead* by Brené Brown (2012)
- *How to Teach Students Who Don't Look Like You: Culturally Responsive Teaching Strategies* by Bonnie Davis (2012)
- *Mindset: The New Psychology of Success* by Carol Dweck (2006)

The Power of Words

To develop greater empathy for others and for ourselves, we engage in fierce and courageous conversations, use powerful words, and ultimately teach our students how to do the same. Bailey (2001) reminds us:

> You cannot teach children the power of words until you have learned it yourself. All teachers, especially women and people of color, must become comfortable with their assertive voices. Generally speaking, people who have historically been disempowered in a culture did not need to develop an assertive voice because society did not allow them to use it. Their voices were simply ignored. Disempowered people tend to believe they must be passive or aggressive to be heard. Assertiveness, however, is the key to communication for *all* people. (p. 100)

Communication has many layers. As Bailey (2001) points out, people who are disempowered often think they must be passive or aggressive if they are to be heard. In the book group, members found that they too often attempted to manage their classrooms from a passive stance, saying such things as: "Students, open your books, okay?" "I'm waiting." "When you're listening, I'll begin." Each of these statements gives learners a choice and attempts to control them through passive language. Also, these messages build codependent relationships with students seeking approval. When students do not obey, the teacher may go from passive to aggressive and express frustration by hollering at students, which leads to guilt, sending the teacher back to the passive mode. This cycle of communication that goes from passive to aggressive back to passive is one groups can discuss, acknowledge, and brainstorm ways to break out of. As Bailey (2001) writes, "To clearly state your thoughts and desires, you must feel entitled to have them, recognize them, and own them. In short, you must value yourself" (p. 100). As a member of a disempowered group, learning to value yourself is not always an easy task, and Bailey (2001) suggests three steps to achieve this:

1. Achieve self-awareness.
2. Monitor your own thought patterns.
3. Teach and utilize assertiveness in all your relationships.

Many people have developed a set of hidden rules that can be attributed to being socialized differently. These hidden rules affect how we communicate and function collaboratively (Bailey, 2001; Gay, 2000; Gilligan, 1982; Tannen, 1990). These hidden rules are an unspoken code of conduct we follow and of which we are often unaware. For example, the following code of conduct is common for white women.

- Be nice.
- Place the needs of others above your own.
- Avoid conflict.
- Do not be direct.
- Expect others to read our minds.

In addition to being *nice*, white women are socialized to maintain the social order and avoid conflict. We do this through being the audience more than the speaker when in groups with white males and by deemphasizing our expertise, and therefore the competition it invokes, in order to avoid any possible conflict. We work to build relationships and intimacy rather than focus on power and conflict (Gay, 2000). If our intent is to avoid conflict, it is difficult to come out from behind ourselves and have fierce or courageous conversations, which, by their very nature, bring out difficult truths. Yet, in order to move from passive behaviors to assertive ones, white women must interrogate the realities of these behaviors and work to change them. Indeed, we must interrogate our communication to ensure we are not being manipulative; we must hold fierce conversations with those who attempt to control us; and we must examine our actions to ensure we are not attempting to control others. In short, we must become culturally literate in our own culture as white women.

White women are unique because we wear the mantle of white privilege but remain part of an oppressed group. This duality is challenging. To meet this challenge, think back to Fullan's (2008) powerful suggestion: love your employees. Unfortunately, there are many stories of sabotage, where white women undo each other's power in an attempt to maintain the status quo. Have you ever heard a white woman say, "I'd rather have a man than a woman for a boss." As white females, we have the power to interrogate reality and learn what we don't know we don't know in order to create a more equitable educational situation for all learners. We discuss more about white female socialization in chapter 6, "Engage in a Cultural Literacy Journey" (page 155), when we describe the cultural literacy journey white female staff members take in their professional and personal lives.

> *Reflect on the hidden rules for white women. With what do you agree and disagree?*
>
> *Think about your language patterns as you work with others—your colleagues and your students. Do you tend to use passive, aggressive, or assertive communication?*

Assertive communication is necessary if we are to interrogate reality and work together on a journey of cultural literacy. Even though our assertive voices may, at first, be uncomfortable, Bailey (2001) writes that we must become comfortable with them to support both our own needs and the needs of others. We become comfortable with our assertive voices through practice and reflection on our practice.

> *Do you speak out about your needs?*
>
> *In what ways do you support others in interrogating the truth in your collaborative conversations?*

By working together in collaborative groups, we are able to have fierce conversations about our beliefs with our peers. Hattie (2012) writes that "teachers' beliefs and commitments are the greatest influences on student achievement *over which we can have some control*" (Kindle location 626). Through these conversations, we share our beliefs and learn that we are not alone, and we can support and learn from each other. As we continue to work together, we expand our identity and commit to a larger picture outside our individual classrooms. One way to get outside our individual classrooms and step into each other's classrooms is to observe learning. This can be done with walkthroughs. In the next section, we describe how to collaborate with this strategy.

Walkthroughs: Stepping Outside the Individual Classroom

Todd Benben began daily walkthroughs the first year he became principal many years ago. Once a day, he walks into each classroom of his school and acknowledges each individual human being, adult and child, by lightly touching him or her on the shoulder. Teachers are so used to his walkthroughs that they do not miss a beat in their instruction. During his daily walkthroughs, Benben is able to gather anecdotal data about students and teachers; he is masterful at sensing classroom climate.

> *What kinds of information do you think he can gather as he walks through classrooms and throughout the school?*

Todd shares that with walkthroughs he can answer questions such as these:

- Are the learners and the teacher relaxed and having fun?
- What appears to be working?
- Is anything not working?
- Are students engaged?
- Is student work displayed on the walls? Is it current and aligned with the lesson?
- Is a particular student not engaged or not included in the lesson? Is there a need to check with this student later?
- Is a teacher upset? Is there a need to check in with the teacher later?

Through this process, Todd gets an understanding of the pulse of the school in a way an administrator who sits in his or her office cannot (T. Benben, personal communication, March 27, 2013).

After years of seeing Todd's walkthroughs, the teachers in his building began their own walkthroughs focused on student learning. As Hattie (2012) writes:

> Teachers need to be aware of what each and every student in their class is thinking and what they know, be able to construct meaning and meaningful experiences in light of this knowledge of the students, and have proficient knowledge and understanding of their subject content so that they can provide meaningful and appropriate feedback such that each student moves progressively through the curriculum levels. (Kindle location 539)

Teacher walkthroughs support this effort as teachers observe how learners are engaged and how they function in classrooms, followed by the opportunity to discuss what they observe in order to apply it in their own practice. In Todd's school, teacher walkthroughs began during the second semester after new teachers had time to become accustomed to the school culture. In *Breaking Through to Effective*

Teaching: A Walk-Through Protocol Linking Student Learning and Professional Practice, Patricia Martinez-Miller and Laureen Cervone (2008) stress the need for learning communities to trust one another. This is one of the reasons to implement teacher walkthroughs—to build on trust and to build more trust among staff.

After Todd introduced the concept of teacher walkthroughs at a staff meeting, some staff followed up with collaborative conversation with mixed results: some staff welcomed the walkthroughs, and others did not support the idea. Some teachers doubted that the strategy was about collecting evidence of learning; instead, they felt it was for additional observations of them, the teachers. Prior observations of teachers tended to be evaluative and focused on teacher instruction, not on student learning—so it was understandable these new walkthroughs threatened and stressed some of the staff. Fortunately, they were able to voice their concerns during the staff meeting rather than in the parking lot. Todd addressed their concerns, and even though not everyone may have felt satisfied at that time, every voice was heard and honored. Walkthroughs would be mandatory, and all classroom teachers were expected to participate.

All classroom teachers participated in the initial round of walkthroughs. Most participated with their grade-level team or their content-specific team. The group of teachers doing the walkthrough met first to determine what it wanted to observe, and that became the target of teachers' observations throughout the walkthrough. Because walkthroughs are content neutral—teachers are not observing for a specific content strategy or lesson—they can be done based on the availability of time of the staff, in this case, during team planning time. Martinez-Miller and Cervone (2008) stress that the following protocol provides "a safe haven in which to rediscover that inquiry drives improvement—to learn that they do have time to learn together because what they learn together results in significantly better student learning and achievement" (pp. 19–20). Staff in Todd's school followed this protocol:

1. Meet in the conference room and decide on a common walkthrough question (ten minutes).
2. Do the walkthroughs—five minutes in each classroom (twenty minutes).
3. Debrief in the conference room (twenty minutes).

Staff used their planning periods to do the walkthroughs. I accompanied them as the facilitator for the work. The schedule for the walkthroughs appears in figure 2.1. Figure 2.2 shows the agenda for the walkthrough.

Day 1:

8:50 a.m. Music, art, librarian—Observe kindergarten

10:00 a.m. Fifth-grade team—Observe third grade

12:15 a.m. Fourth-grade team—Observe first grade

1:50 p.m. First-grade team—Observe second grade

2:40 p.m. Second-grade team—Observe fourth grade

Day 2:

10:50 a.m. Third-grade team—Observe fourth grade

1:00 p.m. Kindergarten team—Observe first grade

Figure 2.1: Sample walkthrough schedule.

1. Meet, decide on question, and go over protocol (ten minutes).
   - Do not use names of teachers or room numbers in your notes or in conversations.
   - Do not take notes while in classrooms—just look for student evidence of learning. (Bring pen and paper to write any notes outside the classrooms.) Pretend you are a video camera, and record only what you see. Do not assume.
   - Take notes pertaining only to your central question.
   - Do not speak to students unless teachers encourage you to speak to students to show evidence of their work.
   - Be quiet and respectful upon entering and leaving the classroom.
2. Perform walkthroughs (twenty minutes).
3. Reflect, process, chart responses, and make notes.

Figure 2.2: Sample walkthrough agenda.

On the day of the walkthroughs, staff members met in the conference room, and each team decided on a question to guide its observations of student learning in classrooms. Some teams used the same guiding question as other teams, while others used different questions. Some possible questions include:

- What language engages students in learning?
- What evidence is there of students' learning?

- What evidence is there of students working together in groups or doing teamwork?

Armed with these questions, teams did their walkthroughs, spending a few minutes in each class. After the walkthroughs, each team gathered in the conference room to list the evidence members observed. Teachers worked in pairs and wrote the evidence on large chart paper that would be hung on the conference room walls. Following is some of the evidence they gathered:

- Kids questioning other kids
- Graphic organizers
- Peer observation form
- Awareness of learning goal and expectations
- Student-centered activities
- Student-to-student conversations and listening to each other
- Focus and calm—teachers who knew what to do!
- Highlighting and underlining information
- Small-group instruction
- Conversation instead of lecture
- Use of technology
- Scaffolded teacher questioning
- Differentiated hands-on activities
- Enjoyment in learning
- Teacher assessing
- Communication that flowed between students and teachers
- Calmness in the learning environment
- Communicating and problem-solving among classmates
- Students showing excitement about books
- Students so engaged they didn't notice being observed
- Sense of community—student of the week, charts, and so on
- Movement—computer, floor, exercise ball, and desk—with attention to different learning styles
- Self-monitoring (checklists)

After listing the evidence, teams discussed any trends in the evidence, which they then wrote on chart paper and posted on the walls. Following are some examples of trends they found:

- Use of technology
- Teacher as learner
- Student-centered lessons
- Students respectful of teacher and other students
- Calm classrooms and learning environments
- Community—charts, posters, student of the week
- Differentiated instruction—small groups, independent learning, paired student, and teacher-led learning
- Evidence of mastery

After listing the trends, teams talked about next steps and listed them on poster paper and displayed them on the walls. Some examples of next steps include the following.

- We would like to do more walkthroughs and see different grade levels.
- We want to continue to affirm learners and learning.
- We want to apply what we saw in class to our own learners.

The final step in the reflective conversations following the walkthroughs is discussion of any final questions. The following were added to poster paper and placed on the wall.

- What can upper-grade teachers use to highlight student mastery?
- How do we apply what we saw?

The walkthroughs have been a powerful way to unite teams and produce fierce conversations. Teachers made comments such as, "I enjoyed the walkthroughs and look forward to more in the future. I would love to spend time in teammates' rooms and kindergarten." However, because many teachers have taught behind closed doors for so many years, for some, walkthroughs may feel like an intrusion. In another district where we did peer observations, teachers were hesitant to walk into their colleagues' rooms. One staff member commented that a teacher's room is like a woman's purse—you don't go into it without permission, and even with permission, it still feels kind of funny. With this in mind, when we decided to visit classrooms in this school, we shifted the paradigm from doing traditional peer observations to doing walkthroughs looking for evidence of student learning. This shift was huge, and it yielded so much more in usable data we could discuss in collaboration and conversations concerning student learning since it was no longer about what teacher A or teacher B does; rather, the focus was on student learning.

It challenged staff members to take the focus away from any feelings of inadequacy and place the focus on the visual evidence of student learning. Too often in the past, staff members compared themselves to each other rather than focusing on student learning. The walkthroughs supported their understanding that the focus is on the learner. It is a shift the staff at the school is still making, but they continue to build trust and yield results.

In addition to walkthroughs, the staff began working with literacy coaches who had previously been the reading specialists for the school. These two women received additional professional development as they made the transition in the district from their roles as reading specialists to their new roles as literacy specialists. These literacy coaches worked together in collaborative conversations to implement a literacy coaching structure that honored staff members' culture and expertise. They demonstrated step 2 of the six-step framework, because literacy coaches and staff members learn together when student learning is their target goal. At the same time, they were including culturally literate practices. These are ongoing professional development opportunities that all staff members engage in throughout the school year.

Literacy Coaching

Roberta McWoods and Vicki Johnson broadened their reading specialist role to combine purposeful coaching for their grade-level teams with their work with struggling readers. They felt a need to support both teachers and struggling readers. It is hard to say where reading support for students and literacy support for teachers begin and end. When you support students, you constantly coach teachers as they learn and grow to meet the needs of their struggling students. However, this new role required the women to expand their approach to better meet the needs of a staff adjusting to differentiation and the CCSS. They decided to do this in a way that respected the staff's expertise and learning curve. They implemented the following seven-step process.

1. Build your own knowledge base. They attended workshops, read research, talked with other literacy leaders, and collaborated about how to coach the staff.

2. Talk with your principal. At the same time they were building their knowledge base, they talked with their principal to establish clarity, a sense of purpose, goals, and a method to ensure they were not going to overwhelm teachers.

3. Give the staff a timeline for literacy coaching. Explain the big picture, goals, timeline, expectations, and outcomes.

4. Meet with each grade-level team once a month during a planning period. Give each team a list of beliefs about literacy instruction. These beliefs about literacy teaching and learning include but are not exclusive to:

- Assessment should be an integral part of teaching and should be used to guide instruction.
- Student writing should be used to teach writing conventions. For example, students should write every day and in every discipline; share their work with peers; use peer editing as a tool in writing to learn; publish; and write multiple drafts leading to a final published piece to be sent home, posted publicly in the school, or sent to a real audience such as a news source.

Ask teachers to rank the beliefs from those they most believe to those they do not believe.

5. Agree on one belief per grade level. Give three or four research articles supporting the belief statement to each team. Ask teachers to read the articles for the next meeting.

6. Discuss with the group what they are doing to support the research and where they feel they need the most improvement. Each team member writes a reflection piece, detailing how well teachers feel they are teaching this belief. Use this during the team discussion. Discuss the next steps and actions to implement before the next meeting.

7. Bring back evidence that supports the team belief statement. Discuss the team's evidence. Discuss how the coaches can help the teachers implement literacy strategies to support the team belief.

We will examine a kindergarten team's belief statement hypothesis and action plan as an example. After the team writes its belief statement in its own language, teachers create a simple action plan to turn the belief statement into action. This is a powerful example of reaching and teaching all learners. The teachers are responsive to the learners' cultures, individual challenges, and group dynamics, including the adult groups in their school. Figure 2.3 (page 54) shows the outline of their plan.

This kindergarten team continues to work on the plan outlined in figure 2.3, and teachers continue to work with their literacy coaches. Even though the school is in its first year of collaboration and conversations using coaches as guides, it has come far. Roberta McWoods, a literacy coach, writes about the process and what makes it work:

> What makes this work is the relationship piece. . . . Because of our relationships as veteran teachers, we were able to understand the strengths and weaknesses of each teacher and worked within their comfort zones. If a coach does not have the luxury of knowing the teachers, I suggest he or she begin by building a relationship first. I think

Grade: Kindergarten

Belief: Assessment should be an integral part of teaching and should be used for guiding instruction.

Hypothesis: If we believe that assessment is an important part of teaching that should be used to guide instruction, then we must first identify ways to involve our students in goal setting, monitoring, and celebrating completed goals. Additionally, we must identify anchor papers that will enable us to consistently assess students' writing.

Action Plan:	Status
1. Place goal on board as a visual reminder for students.	Completed
2. Conduct joint student and teacher goal setting.	Ongoing
3. Reflect on goal work using a rubric with a visual "stoplight."	Ongoing
4. Use a team-generated kindergarten writing prompt.	Completed
5. Gather writing samples based on a prompt.	Completed
6. Determine anchor papers that reflect the rubric standards in progress.	In progress
7. Develop student-friendly rubrics.	In progress

Resources: *6+1 Traits of Writing* by Ruth Culham (2005), rubrics developed by others, and Internet sources

Further Action Items:

1. Continue to develop common assessments.
2. Keep working on in-progress items from the action plan section.
3. Evaluate for effectiveness.

What are your grade level goals?

- To develop writers
- To develop a grade-level rubric
- To establish continuity across our grade level
- To establish high expectations

What is your timeline?

- Meet weekly until completed.
- Our goal is to have this completed by the end of this school year.

Figure 2.3: Sample literacy coaching work for a kindergarten team.

this needs to be established before any of these steps can take place. This relationship is necessary in order for the teachers to trust that what you are asking them to do is what is needed . . . and makes it easier to have the conversations. (personal communication, April 11, 2013)

Vicki Johnson, also a literacy coach, writes about the process:

This approach is effective because we expand our coaching role to meet the needs of the team. This provides a baseline for team discussions, sharing, and team reflections. It prevents a single teacher from feeling he or she owns a problem or is the only one needing help. We felt the hypothesis statements opened the door for honest evaluations of literacy practices. We made it clear from the beginning that we expected teachers to have a product that was developed by the team. We allowed the teams to create reasonable timelines, but provided the accountability and push toward the goal. (personal communication, April 11, 2013)

Roberta and Vicki further comment on what worked with the process. They comment that each team, working with the literacy coach, designed its own professional development experience because it chose its belief statement. This approach created buy-in from the teachers. It was what they felt they most needed. Examples of belief statements included such items as, "Rewrite rubrics, and compile mentor papers that demonstrate each ranking," and "Find books that fill the need for more nonfiction texts, specifically biographies." Roberta and Vicki say that there are things about the process that didn't work. For example, finding time is always a challenge, and holding meetings on time without interruptions from the schedule poses an ongoing challenge. Roberta and Vicki say that after doing one cycle of coaching, they realize they need to help some grade-level teams focus more. They know now that they must adhere to deadlines and require each team member to be responsible for a task at each team meeting. By assigning more specific responsibility to each team member, they receive more buy-in from individual teachers.

In today's educational climate, educators must adopt a big-picture view—learning what we can from collaboration and conversations with others in order to more successfully deliver culturally responsive instruction to all learners.

Conclusion

In this chapter, you saw examples of collaborative conversations among different groups of educators as they attempted to change paradigms as they implement the Common Core State Standards in their classrooms. This attempt to shift paradigms occurred at the onset of the implementation of the Common Core State Standards in this district. Educators focused on their belief system, and once they investigated those beliefs, they explored strategies to support a more rigorous literacy program in the school. All the strategies have one thing in common: educators worked together to explore their experiences as teachers whose main focus is on student learning. The conversations are culturally literate because educators allow for both individual differences and cultural differences for both the students and the teachers. As the teachers learn about themselves and their own cultural behaviors and hidden rules, they are better able to reach out to learners who share their cultures and learners who cross cultures to interact with them. This chapter focuses on teacher collaboration, and even though student collaboration is not addressed in this chapter, it is addressed later in the book. Collaboration is a 21st century skill, and teachers need to provide numerous opportunities for learners in their classrooms to collaborate and grow together. The lessons provided in chapter 5, "Use Feedback to Self-Assess Learning" (page 121), include learner collaboration—a strategy that engages students and extends the learning for all.

Collaborative conversations support educators in continuing to learn what they don't know they don't know. The next chapter introduces you to high-yield, research-based tools and strategies to engage all learners and improve student achievement in your standards-based instruction.

CHAPTER 3

Use High-Yield, Research-Based Strategies

You can change your mindset.

—Carol Dweck

We all want strategies, techniques, and tools that will magically transform students into engaged learners who can't wait to enter our classrooms and master the work. As teachers, we want this so much that, when we have opportunities for professional development, we most often ask for strategies and teaching techniques. Fullan (2008) calls this search for strategies "'techniquey'—seeking tools as solutions instead of getting at the underlying issues" (p. 130). *Techniquey* strategies don't solve problems and bring about change, because there are underlying issues present in schools that prevent students from achieving at their full potential—and we can't solve the problem of low achievement with a single strategy. However, there are strategies and effective teaching tools that do influence student learning and support the implementation of the Common Core State Standards, and research (Hattie, 2012) provides a list of the most effective ones, some of which we examine in this chapter. Too often we are trying our best, but we are not using the most effective high-yield, research-based learning strategies. To influence student learning, we need to choose and refine strategies, techniques, and tools that are proven by the research to make a difference.

> *How is using high-yield, research-based strategies any different from what you have done in the past?*

In this chapter, we examine some of the most effective strategies teachers can incorporate into their planning and delivery of lessons. Of course, there are many more possible strategies. Hattie (2012) states that any strategy might work for any teacher in his or her classroom and influence learning, but that same strategy may not have been proven to be effective across classrooms.

> *What teaching strategies do you find most effective?*
>
> *What evidence do you use that shows they are effective?*

Many things influence student learning. Some are beyond the control of educators—prior knowledge and achievement, home environment, and socioeconomic status, for example. However, many others fall under teachers' control and are directly tied to learning. Results from Hattie's (2012) meta-analyses of more than nine hundred research studies reveal what most influences student achievement. Some of the significant influences are self-reported grades and student expectations, response to intervention, classroom discussion, feedback, the teacher-student relationship, meta-cognitive strategies, providing goals, teacher clarity, and vocabulary. Of these, several, such as goal setting and vocabulary instruction, are also found on the list of strategies compiled from the research of Robert Marzano, Debra Pickering, and Katie Pollock (2001). Many of these would be considered culturally responsive since they build relationships with students, signal that teachers have high expectations for students, and offer needed background information, such as academic vocabulary, to ensure student academic success.

In addition to those mentioned already, cooperative learning is another influential strategy emphasized in this chapter and found in the teacher narratives throughout the book. It is a culturally responsive strategy suggested by Geneva Gay, an expert in culturally responsive instruction. Gay (2000) writes that incorporating cooperative learning opportunities speaks to the fact that "underlying values of human connectedness and collaborative problem solving are high priorities in the cultures of most groups of color in the United States," and it also speaks to the "communicative, procedural, motivational, and relational dimensions" of these groups' learning styles (p. 158). Since collaborative problem solving is a high priority for most groups of color in the United States, learning in cooperative groups is an example of a culturally responsive classroom practice.

Lisa Delpit (2012) agrees, noting that "culturally sensitive classroom life should also include collaboration and group interaction in the name of academic achievement" and that "students report that a classroom culture of cooperation and collaboration also makes it easier to engage because they feel more secure and less vulnerable" (p. 188). This collaboration and group interaction offers ample opportunities for student visibility and voice while it creates a classroom that supports the practices reinforced by many cultures. When teachers incorporate student collaboration and group interaction, they are being culturally literate in their practice (and most learners want to work with peers, too). As teachers get to know their students and student cultures, they can make more deliberate decisions about classroom instruction and practice and implement the strategies reinforced positively by the cultures of the learners in their classrooms. This creates the environment needed for the rigor the Common Core State Standards demand. Learners, in this kind of collaborative environment, are not left to struggle alone, but, instead, can work with others in collaboration to engage in standards-based instruction.

How Do We Think About Strategies?

Do we as teachers deliberately think about the strategies we employ within our instruction and why we have chosen specific strategies for the lesson we are teaching? Jane Pollock (2012) tells us that "teachers are the most important factor in student success, but only if they deliberately use teaching practices to change students' low performances" (p. 17). These teaching practices, or strategies, must be applied deliberately, and they must focus on learning. This represents a shift in thinking from teaching to learning. Pollock (2012) reminds us that rather than focusing on teaching strategies, which is what teachers seem to want, we need to flip the focus to learning strategies. In *Feedback: The Hinge That Joins Teaching and Learning* (Pollock, 2012) and *Minding the Achievement Gap: One Classroom at a Time* (Pollock, Ford, & Black, 2012), we find strategies that do just that. Pollock and her colleagues focus on learning rather than teaching to improve student achievement. They studied positive deviant students— those students who did better than their peers and beat the odds in seemingly difficult situations. They identified three characteristics of these positive deviant students: (1) they knew how to find the learning goal of every lesson, (2) they used high-yield strategies, and (3) they sought feedback (Pollock et al., 2012).

These three characteristics of successful students support them in mastering tasks—in other words, in learning the goal of every lesson. If teachers want to support all students in mastering tasks, the authors conclude that teachers need to effect three critical changes in their students:

1. Student awareness of goals and success criteria,

2. student use of high-yield strategies in active pursuit of learning, and

3. student pursuit and use of feedback to guide that learning to a successful outcome. (Pollock et al., 2012, p. 29)

In addition, Pollock (2012) suggests we need to shift our focus from being "'master teachers' to creating 'master learners'" (p. 48). How do we choose the strategies that fit the learners in our classrooms? We must begin with a "deep understanding of what each student already knows and can do, and how the instruction is aimed at increasing the progress and levels of achievement for each of the students," writes Hattie (2012, Kindle location 969). We must learn the ways of thinking, Hattie (2012) adds, as we make the shift from master teachers to creating master learners. Throughout this chapter, you will find teachers who teach their students the ways of thinking or metacognitive strategies to support their learning. Giving students these tools is an example of shifting from being master teachers to creating master learners. It is also culturally responsive since it levels the playing field, giving all learners the tools they need to succeed. This shift from being master teachers to creating master learners aligns with the emphasis of the CCSS because teachers have the task of equipping learners for college and career readiness. One way to equip learners for college and career readiness is to teach learners how to set goals.

Goal Setting

Goal setting is the process of establishing a direction for learning (Marzano et al., 2001). On Hattie's list of influences, goal setting shows a large effect size on achievement. Hattie (2012) writes, "The more transparent the teacher makes the learning goals, the more likely the student is to engage in the work needed to meet the goal. Also, the more the student is aware of the criteria of success, the more the student can see and appreciate the specific actions that are needed to attain these criteria" (Kindle location 1115). In education, the use of goal setting continues to evolve from simply having students write down a goal to ensuring that they understand the goal at the beginning of the lesson. Hattie (2012) identifies two parts to targeted learning: first, teachers must be clear about what is to be learned from the lesson—the learning target or intention; and second, teachers need a way to know the learning has been achieved. The shift in goal setting from teacher to students occurs when the pathways to success are transparent for the student, which builds trust between the teacher and the learner so students engage more in the learning as they move toward the learning target (Hattie, 2012).

Another shift needed to encourage goal setting is supporting students in connecting the learning target to their own lives. In *Minding the Achievement Gap: One Classroom at a Time*, Pollock et al. (2012) point out that, in the past, teachers may have asked students to write down a goal for the day, but now they are providing "the opportunity for students to understand the goals and to personalize them" (p. 22). Connecting the goal to their own lives supports culturally responsive instruction and cultural literacy. In the following piece, Jean Ducey shares how she and the kindergarten team in her school teach goal setting within the context of a literacy lesson aligned to the CCSS.

We named ourselves the "K Team Chicks": five passionate kindergarten teachers along a wide spectrum of experience. We work together as a cohesive team, planning, supporting and aligning our curriculum with the CCSS. Here is a glimpse of how goal setting naturally unfolded in my classroom, Team Ducey, as a result of this collaboration.

In the early weeks of school, we focused significantly on building our stamina. After a 5–8 minute minilesson uncovering how good writers write about things they know, we set to work. Our goal is to become stronger writers each day—to write longer than we did the day before. With daily diligence and joy, we celebrated big once we hit our stamina goal of 20 minutes! Morale was high among the writers in the class. We emailed pictures of ourselves writing to our parents; we shared our work with a partner for feedback and encouragement.

While stamina had increased, quality had not. The team knew it was time to present this issue to our writers. We needed to give them the chance to look at their progress and assess where to go next. My teammate, Trisha, had an idea to find a common focus that would entice change: illustrations. This would allow students to still keep their writing stamina, while still subtly turning their direction to become accountable to their audience.

We created a rubric with a four-point scale, showing gradually how detail and attention to color can really tell a story and grab the audience.

We spent careful time over the course of several minilessons unfolding this tool. Every writer received a copy of the rubric for his or her writing folder, and we had a large one hanging in the front of our room as an anchor chart. I began asking individual writers if I could borrow their illustrations for the debrief at the end of each lesson. As a writing community, within the safety of our established team, we were able to examine the work of our friends under the document camera and critique their illustrations against our rubric. We compared this reflection to the work of former Cardinal baseball player Albert Pujols. When he was in a hitting slump, he would videotape his swing to see what he needed to do better to hit balls out of Busch Stadium. His coaches and friends gave him tips and ideas. If he could do this and learn, so could we. The impact of our rubric work was magnetic. . . . Everyone was attracted to it. We used the stem, "I wonder if . . ." to keep our feedback positive and promote creative thinking. We learned that we can all always do better. I also jumped in as both a learner and a teacher. I would daily share my journey as a runner with my writers, and let them know how I would set goals to always improve my form, my enjoyment, and my health!

As a team, we also met monthly with our literacy coaches. Collaboratively, we began to discuss the work we had been doing with writing. We wanted to continue the momentum we started with the illustration rubrics, and so, a new question evolved: If our writers can use a rubric to set goals for their illustrations, can we get them to do this same kind of work with the conventions of print? So we began with the end in sight. We spoke as a team about what conventions we needed to hold our writers accountable for as they left our kindergarten rooms in May. (personal communication, January 15, 2013)

These kindergarten students learned to become stronger writers by setting goals and working hard to reach them. They connected the work to their own lives by emailing to their parents pictures of themselves writing in class. They shared their work with their peers and received feedback. Finally, they used an illustration rubric for their stories. As a result of the metacognition about the learning in their classrooms, the teachers formulated a question to present to the literacy coaches based on the use of the illustration rubric. They met with their literacy coaches and set goals for the work throughout the year, deciding on what conventions they would hold their writers accountable for at the end of the year. Both teachers and students were learners who used high-yield, research-based strategies, such as goal setting and metacognition, to improve student writing at the kindergarten level. Goal setting, and the consistent feedback from students and colleagues, allowed the teachers to implement the Common Core State Standards and give students tools to guide their learning throughout their lives. By giving the students tools to become lifelong learners, the teachers engaged in culturally responsive instruction.

SMART Goals*

Anyone reading about goals in today's educational literature will come across a particular kind of goal called a SMART goal. The SMART goal acronym (Conzemius & O'Neill, 2006) provides a concise and useful framework for examining behavior as well as setting action goals for improvement. Goals are SMART when they are:

- Strategic and specific
- Measurable
- Attainable
- Results oriented
- Time bound (setting a specific time when the goal will be achieved)

Mary Kim Schreck has spent years in New Mexico helping teachers get their minds around the shifts required to implement the Common Core State Standards. One tool that is proving valuable is the use of SMART goals for examining behavior as well as setting action goals for improvement. The following is an example of a SMART goal that focuses on teacher goal setting, rather than student goal setting. While implementing the CCSS, teachers are being asked to allow students to struggle in their learning—instead of immediately helping a student at the first sign of confusion. Teachers are urged to give students the opportunity to work at figuring out the problem or text by themselves—to experience the challenge, the effort at working out the dilemma before receiving help. This leads to far deeper learning and construction of the growth mindset that is so necessary for mastering higher-order thinking skills. As a teacher, do you provide opportunities for students to deal with their frustration over a text? Do you rush to help a struggling student or smooth the learning path so that there are no bumps? The following sample activity uses SMART goals to help you determine if you have an impulse to over-help students or if you actually allow them to grapple with difficulty. Begin by formulating a SMART goal. The following goal is similar to the way Margaret C. Wang, Geneva D. Haertel, and Herbert J. Walberg (1993) describe SMART goal construction:

---

* My colleague and author Mary Kim Schreck contributed this section on SMART goals.

Because I will consciously keep from providing help to my students on every assignment and allow them more time and opportunity to practice tolerating frustration, 80 percent of my students are aware that they are tolerating frustration when they first begin a difficult text. By the end of two weeks, 80 percent will report back to me in writing that they are not jumping for help immediately but are holding off until after they try to do the task themselves.

The sample SMART goal covers all the requirements for a valid and workable SMART goal. (1) It is strategic and specific—its focus is on allowing more time for students to tolerate their frustration over the work they are doing. (2) It is measurable; the percentage of students who at this point should be aware of their own efforts at tolerating frustration is 80 percent. (3) It is attainable; the teacher feels this percentage can be met. (4) It is results orientated; students will report back to the teacher in writing concerning their behavior when confronting difficult material or demands. And (5) it is time bound; two weeks is the deadline the teacher gives to achieve the results.

Use a chart such as the example in figure 3.1 to measure your progress toward meeting your SMART goals.

Class Period	Student (Asking for your help)	Your Response (Wait, go help, or urge student to try again)	Time (Amount you waited before helping out)	Comment (On how this felt, or how it went)

Figure 3.1: Sample chart for measuring a SMART goal.

Metacognitive Strategies

Hattie (2012) states that using metacognitive strategies is very powerful in influencing student achievement. *Metacognitive strategies* are methods used to help students understand the way they learn and to think about their thinking. *Metacognition* means "big thinking," and teachers can guide learners in using metacognitive strategies such as questioning, visualizing, and synthesizing information to examine their thinking processes as they learn. Throughout this chapter, teachers share how they use metacognitive strategies such as making connections, predictions, or inferences; thinking aloud; and doing others within the context of their lessons. Also, throughout this book, you will find reflection questions that support you in your own process of metacognition as you use the six-step framework to guide your instruction. Understanding the impact of metacognition, how can we use metacognitive strategies during instruction? Consider the following questions.

> *Do you ask students to reflect on their work?*
>
> *Do you post metacognitive questions on the walls of your classroom?*
>
> *Do you use metacognitive strategies, such as sharing your thinking with students, to model the learning process?*

Learners can be taught to *metacognate*—to think about their own thinking. In her book *Mindset: The New Psychology of Success*, Carol Dweck (2006) describes two different kinds of mindsets that come into play when implementing metacognitive strategies: *fixed mindset*, the belief that intelligence is fixed and you either have it or not, and *growth mindset*, the belief that the mind is capable of changing, growing, and continually learning. Her work suggests that we have a choice about what to think with our minds. In addition, teachers can explicitly teach mindset to the learners in their classrooms.

The teaching of mindset is important for all learners, but it is especially relevant to minority and lower-achieving students. Hattie (2012) finds that minority and lower-achieving students are "less accurate in their self-estimates or self-understanding of achievement. They tend to underestimate their achievement and, over time, they come to believe their lower estimates and lose the confidence to take on more challenging tasks" (Kindle location 1327). The research is sobering about what can happen if teachers do not attend to their students' predictions of their academic performance. Hattie (2012) states that "changing these students' predictions of their performance has proved to be very difficult, often because this lower confidence and learned helplessness has developed and been reinforced over a long time" (Kindle location 1327). To break the cycle of learned helplessness and get these students on the right track for college and career readiness, we can teach them how to develop growth mindsets. Ideally, this would begin with younger learners, and that is just what several first-grade teachers at North Glendale Elementary School in Kirkwood, Missouri, do in their classrooms. For the past two years, they have worked in collaboration to design lessons to teach mindset to their students and reflected together on the process of teaching metacognitive strategies. One first-grade team member, teacher Sabrina Skinner, shares her observations:

> I believe that by teaching the concept of growth and fixed mindsets I created motivation and strengthened relationships within our community. I was incredibly impressed with how my students grasped the concept so quickly and truly understood how important it was to have and keep a growth mindset. They would say, "With a fixed mindset, we are stuck in the mud." Their favorite growth mindset phrase seems to be, "This is hard, but I will try." It is so amazing to me how often I hear kids telling their friends, "You can do it!" when they see that they are becoming frustrated with something. We have a mural in our classroom with the kids' fixed mindset phrase "bricks" on the bottom, first grade goal "flowers" in the middle, and growth mindset phrase "clouds" about the "flowers." There is also a yellow sun with a caption that says, "With a growth mindset we can do ANYTHING!" (personal communication, February 3, 2013)

Following is a lesson Sabrina created to teach mindset to her learners.

Sabrina begins by asking students to read *Unique Monique* by Maria Rousaki (2008) on day one. (Other possible titles include *Thank You, Mr. Faulkner, How Full Is Your Bucket?, Winners Never Quit,* and *Pete the Cat* books.) She explains that *growth mindset* is the belief that you can change and become smarter. How well you can do something depends on how hard you work at it. Your brain is a muscle that needs to be trained. Take risks and embrace challenges because you'll become stronger! A fixed mindset, she explains, is the belief that you are born with a certain ability level and you cannot change or get better at things. You are the way you are. You don't take risks because you don't want to fail.

Students then add to a flip chart in two columns: fixed versus growth mindsets, as in the example in figure 3.2.

Once students brainstorm their lists, Sabrina closes the discussion by asking, "Which mindset does Unique Monique have? How do you know? What mindset will help you be more successful? Why?"

The next day, students read *Wilma Unlimited* by Kathleen Krull (2000). Sabrina asks students, "What mindset is shown in the book? How do you know?" Students refer back to their chart from the previous day.

On the next day, students read *Amazing Grace* by Mary Hoffman and Caroline Binch (1991). Sabrina asks, "What mindset is shown in the book? How do you know?" Students then compare a fixed mindset to a brick: a brick is hard, and you cannot change it. They compare a growth mindset to a cloud: a cloud is soft and can shape easily. They refer back to the chart before the students write a fixed mindset on a red piece of paper in the shape of a brick and a growth mindset on a white piece of paper in the shape of a cloud. Students then place their bricks and clouds on a wall as reminders of fixed and growth mindsets. Figure 3.3 shows students' positive mindset statements written on clouds.

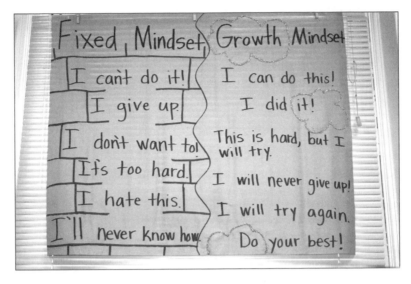

Figure 3.2: Sample fixed versus growth mindsets chart.

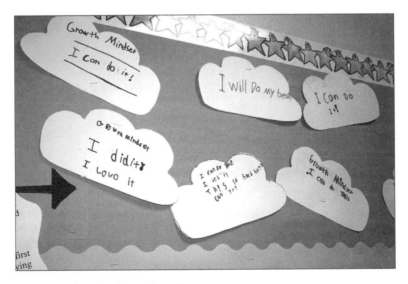

Figure 3.3: Growth mindset clouds.

Teachers can extend the lesson with other ways for students to reinforce the material, such as having students sit in a circle while each child says a growth mindset statement into a microphone. These growth mindset statements can be statements found on the clouds and bricks, or they can be original statements made by the learners. The teacher refers to the clouds and bricks when needed.

Elizabeth Stickley, another teacher on the same first-grade team, began using mindset strategies and metacognition after hearing about it from Sabrina. She shares how the team worked together through their collaborative conversations to grow their students' minds.

One day when my students did rocket math, I overheard a student say, "I can't do this, it's too hard." We took a break from what we were doing and headed straight for Miss Skinner's room to see her mindset wall.

I first reminded my students of our first grade motto: "Think you can, try hard, stay smart." We talked about why those words were our motto and about what they mean. I shared about how Miss Skinner's friends made a visual to help remember our motto, and I shared what some of the bricks said. I asked my students to share if any of them have felt the same way—like they couldn't do something or they weren't good at something and wanted to give up. I raised my hand and almost my entire class did too. We talked about being stuck in a fixed mindset, but we acknowledged that if we think we can and try hard, we are closer to getting to our goal than not trying at all! When we have a growth mindset, anything can happen.

We brainstormed some more words that we could put in clouds—to demonstrate our growth mindset in regards to rocket math. Then we went back to our classroom and persevered during rocket math. Then, after the practice and one-minute quiz, I heard the same student say, "I still didn't get my goal, but it is okay because I tried hard and I got more than I did yesterday. Maybe I will get my goal tomorrow." What a great illustration of how one student's mindset changed with a short, impromptu teachable moment.

Before I began the mindset study with my students, I thought about actually quitting rocket math in my classroom, even though I believe it is essential that first graders become proficient and automatic with basic math facts and number sense as a foundation for higher-level math. But now, I am glad I do it because I feel like it is my job and duty to actually teach kids how to deal with failure (along with successes), because failure is a part of life. If we know how to deal with failure, how to try again, how to get back on the horse, that lesson is one that will keep on giving. Kids need to be taught how to deal with times when they don't succeed. (personal communication, February 15, 2013)

One of the strengths of using mindset strategies is that students can use them in multiple ways. The metacognitive thinking that mindset teaches causes students to reflect on their learning. In addition, the strategies teach students responsible behaviors, such as persistence on a task, underscoring that mistakes and failure are parts of learning. They also can help students understand that some learning and some tasks are more difficult than others, and it is okay to work long and hard to understand a concept and master a skill. All together, mindset teaches students to reflect on their learning, to monitor their behaviors, and to maintain a positive stance while engaging in rigorous work. In the next section, the teacher uses mindset to teach students to persevere in their academics as well as modify their behaviors.

Whitney Coombs, a third member of the elementary team and a first-year teacher in the building, shares her reflections. Like many teachers, Whitney had some students who exhibited behavior problems in her classroom. She wanted to not only relate growth mindsets to persevering in academics but also to improving behavior.

One particular student came into my class at the beginning of the school year with a bad reputation and a fixed mindset that her negative behavior could not improve. She was very defiant, did not listen or have respect for authority, had daily temper tantrums, and was mean to other students. Although smart, her behavior was holding her back academically.

One of my goals in teaching this student about mindsets was to help her realize that her behavior is in her control and that she can change it. During every minilesson I taught the importance of having a growth mindset and read a book that showed how having a growth mindset helped people to accomplish amazing things. My students' favorite book on this subject is Wilma Unlimited: How Wilma Rudolph Became the World's Fastest Woman *by Kathleen Krull (2000). This book really resonated with my students, and I still use Wilma's story as a motivation to persevere. In the nonfiction book, Wilma had polio and was told that she would never walk again. She refused to have a fixed mindset and kept doing her leg exercises. She believed that if she tried hard enough that she could walk one day. Wilma's incredible growth mindset not only gave her the perseverance and determination to walk, but also led her to becoming the first American woman to win three gold medals at one Olympics.*

With every book we read, we had a class discussion on different situations in which we have had a growth mindset (for example, learning to ride a bike) and what it enabled us to accomplish. I include in each discussion about growth mindset how it can help us behaviorally, in the hope that the discussion would strike an encouraging note with my defiant, fixed mindset student. Whenever I noticed that the particular student was on the verge of having a temper tantrum, I would remind her how she could have a growth mindset and realize that she had the power and ability to change her behavior. I saw improvements in her behavior very soon after! She still has a lot of progress to make, but she is a completely different student than she was at the beginning of the school year. (personal communication, February 22, 2013)

These three teachers used objects from their students' experiences (bricks and clouds) to model metacognitive strategies for learners. The teachers have developed growth mindsets themselves as they share strategies with each other and keep themselves open to new ideas. No longer are teachers closing doors and separating themselves from others; instead, these teachers are having fierce conversations about what they and their students need to achieve at their highest potentials. When teachers engage in these fierce conversations and open their classroom doors, they are practicing cultural literacy. They are exhibiting the willingness to be vulnerable, make mistakes, learn from others, and change their practice. They are responding to the individual and cultural needs of their students by using high-yield, metacognitive strategies that build student efficacy and create equitable classrooms for all learners. By teaching students these metacognitive strategies, teachers create a classroom where they can increase rigor and effectively teach the Common Core State Standards in an environment where every learner is expected to grow and attain success.

Teachers not only need to teach their students about a growth mindset but also use the growth mindset language every day. The teachers featured in this section accomplish this by posting growth mindset statements on the walls of their classrooms and refer to them throughout the day. When they hear a student utter a fixed-mindset statement, such as, "I can't do this, it's too hard," they stop, point to the growth mindset statement on the wall, and ask the student to say, "This is hard, but I will try." These teachers help the learners to equip themselves with metacognitive strategies to use throughout their lives as they continue their school journeys. Todd Benben, the principal at North Glendale, shares his thoughts on the implementation of mindset at the school:

> With the introduction of mindset, our teachers, students, and parents are re-examining their own thought processes and patterns. We are trying to teach a new way of thinking. Many times it is easier to establish those thinking patterns when students are younger, before the "fix" sets in. In order for us to teach this concept, we must, ourselves, examine our own mindset and lead by example, demonstrating a growth mindset in all that we do with our students. (personal communication, February 20, 2013)

To illustrate how Todd models the mindset mentality, here is a comment from his weekly bulletin (Benben, 2013):

> All of your continued incredible daily instruction has made a huge difference with your students. Please do not overly stress over the upcoming MAP testing (Missouri state tests). We have proven that through hard work, excellent interventions, quality teaching and lessons, practice, attention to detail, and a growth mindset, anything is possible. I am already proud of you. Remember that your class takes on your personality and follows your lead. If you are calm, cool and relaxed, they will be that way also. Your positivity and enthusiasm is contagious! (p. 2)

The school's test scores illustrate the staff's effectiveness in using high-yield, research-based strategies to equip learners with skills to succeed as they continue their education and graduate into life. The decision by the first-grade team to be purposeful and explicitly teach the mindset strategies is an example of teachers' own metacognition. They knew with the implementation of the Common Core State Standards that their learners needed tools to support the increase in rigor the standards demanded. They discussed and reflected on their needs and the needs of their learners and then decided to incorporate the use of mindset strategies within their classroom instruction. The students learned to metacognitively think about their own thinking and make decisions to use a positive mindset when engaged in rigorous work. The teachers emphasized metacognition throughout their daily instruction and asked students to use strategies such as making predictions, questioning, and visualizing their own learning process as they engaged in meaningful work.

> *After reading how the team taught metacognitive strategies to their first graders, what are your ideas for implementing mindset strategies?*

Academic Language

In addition to teaching mindset, the first-grade team at North Glendale purposely teaches academic language. *Academic language* is the language used in textbooks, in classrooms, and on tests. It differs from the everyday spoken language of social situations. Since the Common Core State Standards incorporate academic language in the standards, students must be able to read and understand the language. In order to read and understand academic language, students must be taught an academic vocabulary consistent with the expectations for their grade levels. This happens during vocabulary study. Hattie (2012) lists vocabulary study as having a significant influence on achievement; therefore, the first-grade team searched for ways to embed vocabulary study within instruction. For example, Lindsay Carleton and Robert Marzano (2010) identify thirteen different types of games teachers can use to teach academic vocabulary that can be adapted to almost any subject or grade level.

After examining numerous ways to teach vocabulary, the teachers on the first-grade team at North Glendale developed an academic vocabulary booklet to use to teach academic language. According to team member Barb Swalina, the academic vocabulary booklet evolved after a district committee of teachers from grades K–5, including special school district-related services personnel, met to compile a list of curriculum-specific "words to know" for each grade level. The first-grade team created the original booklet from the list of words that were deemed most important—for example, those curriculum-specific academic vocabulary words and their meanings that all first graders should know. Barb explains how she incorporates the academic vocabulary booklets in her classroom:

> I do not have a formal lesson plan that I use to teach the words. I introduce each word by bringing it up on the ActivBoard. We talk about the word and its meaning. Together we brainstorm what the word looks like and how we can use the word in a sentence in our academic vocabulary booklets. I let students describe to their peers how they plan to use the word in a sentence and what their picture will look like. With

academic vocabulary journals in hand, students return to their tables. Each student uses the academic word in a sentence and draws a picture on the designated page in his or her journal.

This past summer in a grade-level meeting with our literacy coach, we realized that some of the academic vocabulary words were so embedded in the curriculum that we needed to shift our efforts to true academic vocabulary: words that need to be taught explicitly. Many of the content-specific words were pulled out and replaced with challenging literacy and mathematics Common Core State Standards words. (personal communication, February 23, 2013)

Posters showing the academic vocabulary are clearly visible in every classroom, and each student is expected to master the academic vocabulary before he or she leaves first grade. Figure 3.4 and figure 3.5 (page 74) show examples of academic vocabulary booklets and posters of academic vocabulary from a first-grade classroom.

Figure 3.4: Sample page from an academic vocabulary notebook.

Figure 3.5: Sample academic vocabulary poster.

In addition to the lists of academic vocabulary and the academic vocabulary note-books, the team compiled a list of websites to supplement their academic vocabulary study:

- www.wordle.net
- www.visuwords.com
- www.jeopardylabs.com
- www.vocabahead.com
- http://quizlet.com

The team members understand the importance of academic vocabulary, know-ing that the learners in their classrooms must be able to read and understand the language of textbooks and tests. They work to build a strong foundation by explic-itly teaching vocabulary, one of the strongest influences on student achievement according to the research (Hattie, 2012). In addition to metacognitive strategies and academic vocabulary, students need to learn critical-thinking skills.

In what ways do you teach academic vocabulary to your learners?

Critical-Thinking Skills

In *How to Teach Thinking Skills Within the Common Core: 7 Key Student Proficiencies of the New National Standards*, authors James Bellanca, Robin Fogarty, and Brian Pete (2012) stress the necessity of teaching critical thinking. They state that critical thinking is the "brick and mortar of problem solving and decision making," adding that "for those who hope to advance their education beyond high school and into college or to compete for a significant job in the new global economy, the ability to think critically is a well-recognized imperative and an essential part of this century's first set of Common Core State Standards" (p. 13). Critical thinking is the intentional application of rational, higher-order thinking skills. Metacognition is often defined as a characteristic of critical thinking. When learners use critical-thinking skills, they engage in such thinking as analysis, synthesis, problem recognition, and problem solving, inference, and evaluation. These are also the thinking skills we employ when we practice culturally responsive instruction. Being culturally literate asks that we analyze and evaluate our own biases, that we hold high expectations for students from all cultures and do not allow stereotypical thinking to lower our expectations for all learners in our classrooms. It is just as important that our students learn to do the same.

Delpit (2012) writes, "The urgent need for demanding critical thinking of our students exists in all subject areas. Only those who are authentically and critically literate can become the independently thinking citizens required for any society's evolution" (p. 128). And for all of those people who object to their children learning how to think critically and question authority, Delpit (2012) writes, "Although we sometimes seem to act to the contrary, there is no real dichotomy between teaching 'basic skills' and insisting that children learn to think critically'" (p. 135). A culturally literate teacher teaches both the basic skills and the skills of critical thinking.

In the following section, Christina Steffen shares her experience with teaching critical-thinking skills in a culture that differed dramatically from her own. She attended a workshop held at her school featuring Robert Swartz, director of the National Center for Teaching Thinking. He presented the *infusion method*—a blending of critical-thinking skills into content instruction that aids in students' internalization of specific content material (Swartz, 2007).

Teachers then developed lessons using critical-thinking skills infused into their content discipline. Six weeks later, Swartz returned to meet with the teachers before they presented their lessons. He then observed the lessons and coached teachers in a post conference. Christina shares her experience.

I was one of those teachers. To say it changed my life sounds so simple. It transformed my life. It was one of the top-five pivotal experiences that changed everything. It changed me personally, and it changed the way I thought about teaching. It gave me a voice that resonates today with my students in and out of the classroom. This transformation didn't happen overnight. I am still growing as a learner, and every day I use the skills of critical and creative thinking.

I was an art teacher, that's why I think I felt I didn't know how to be a critical thinker. . . . I thought I was a creative thinker! One might think that I should have known—after all aren't teachers supposed to be critical thinkers? What I learned was how to think. Think like an artist and understand what it means to think like a mathematician, a scientist, or even a historian.

Through a series of events spanning several years, I was asked by Dr. Swartz to help him at a university in Jeddah, Saudi Arabia. I first traveled there in 2006. Men weren't allowed on the women's campus, where I observed how the teachers utilized critical-thinking skills in their lesson development and teaching.

Before I left for Jeddah, I was briefed about some of the culture and traditions that I would encounter. I really didn't know what to expect or see, so I had no preconceived ideas or opinions. What I learned was how different, yet how much the same, we all are. The first time I observed one of the professors, she was giving a lesson on dental amalgams. Some of the lessons were in Arabic, while some were in English. This one was in Arabic so my interpreter, Fatimah, described how she was using a decision-making thinking map. The professor broke the class into groups so the students could discuss the pros and cons of using an amalgam versus other dental materials. At that point, the students became very excited and were lively talking, asking each other questions, and discussing the lesson. At the conclusion of the class, the professor brought the students back together and asked them what kind of thinking they just engaged in, how they might use that kind of thinking in other situations, and how they liked using the thinking map. All the students responded by saying they wanted all their lessons taught this way.

After the class left, Fatimah and I sat down with the professor to talk about the lesson. When I asked her how she thought the lesson went, she told us that she never experienced such excitement and that she was totally surprised by the students' reaction. We learned she never tried group work or simply walked around the classroom talking to her students and asking them questions. She listened to her students and, as I found out later, she changed her teaching practices.

Over the course of a few days, I observed many other teachers giving lessons in other subjects using critical-thinking skills. But one lesson at an elementary school stood out to me. The principal gave a lesson using parts to whole. She started the lesson (ages four to five) by holding up her hand and asking the children what it was (the whole part). The children said, "Your hand" in English. Then she held up her little finger (one of the parts) and the children happily said, "Your little finger." The principal worked through the lesson asking the children what would happen if a particular "part" were missing and what the function of the "part" was, until finally, she asked them to think about their thinking (using the same questions as above from the amalgam lesson). She didn't need to probe for answers. Her students readily jumped into a rich discussion that resulted in the children giving examples from their own lives. They saw and felt the connection. The hand lesson was a model for a future lesson on the parts of a story.

Over and over again I saw the same electrifying engagement from teachers and students. What seemed to be a simple lesson in critical thinking became a new beginning that opened up a new world of best practices. The interaction of teachers and students reminded me that building relationships across all cultures is of utmost importance in a global society. The teachers that I observed connected with their students in ways they never had before.

I went back to Saudi Arabia one more time in 2007. Fatimah was again my interpreter, but I discovered I didn't need one. All I needed to do was watch and listen. Understanding and learning was happening no matter what language was being spoken. It taught me that there are no barriers in education, only a desire for deep thinking, learning, and understanding. (C. Steffen, personal communication, April 13, 2013)

Christina was able to use her own critical-thinking skills as she shared with women eager to learn and implement what they learned. In addition, she observed other culturally responsive instructional strategies. She observed the teacher building relationships through personal interaction with her students and connecting the learning to the students' lives. She observed the collaborative nature of learning; even though the class was in Arabic, a language she did not understand, she understood that learning was taking place by watching the interaction of the teacher and the learners.

It can be simple to connect learning to students' lives. Before you begin a new lesson, consider how you might make a direct connection to the students in your class. We all share basic needs, and that can be one place to begin. Once you know how you are going to make connections to students' lives, you can select critical-thinking strategies to include in the lesson. In the lessons in this section, the instructors chose decision-making thinking maps and a parts-to-whole lesson. In the next chapter, you will find lessons that use critical-thinking skills to investigate issues of social justice.

> *In what ways might you apply critical-thinking skills in your instruction?*

Student-Supported Strategies

There are additional strategies teachers can use during instruction to build relationships and engage learners. In the Chapel Hill-Carrboro City School District, Graig Meyer, Curtis Linton, Dorothy Kelly, and I gave a group of high school students a list of fifteen strategies and asked the students to choose the six they most wanted their teachers to use during instruction. These adolescents were all students of color and participants in the district's award-winning program, the Blue Ribbon Mentor-Advocate Program. (For more on this program, see chapter 6, page 155.) This project, which we titled The Student Six, was filmed by The School Improvement Network (2011) and published on its website (www.schoolimprovement.com) as part of the PD 360 video series. The students' list of their top six are visibility; proximity; connecting to students' lives; engaging students' cultures; addressing race; and connecting to students' future lives. In chapter 1, we extensively discuss visibility. Throughout the book, we discuss connecting to students' cultures and lives. In the following section, we examine proximity. We believe these strategies are important to include since they build relationships and connect students to the teacher and to each other. They are culturally responsive strategies since they establish the collaborative culture in the classroom stressed by Delpit (1995) and Gay (2000). This collaborative culture reduces stress and threat and creates a place conducive to the implementation of the Common Core State Standards (Davis, Kelly, Meyer, & Chapel Hill-Carrboro City School District, 2011).

Proximity

Latino/Latina and African American high school juniors and seniors in the Students' Six Project shared some interesting thoughts with us during interviews when it came to proximity. These students shared that they wanted their teachers to be near them physically when they taught new content. One high school student explicitly stated that he learned better when he could sit next to the teacher. Even though proximity is a culturally responsive strategy when the proximity is initiated to build relationships and trust between teacher and students, it can also be used as a classroom-management technique to quell off-task behavior. Because we sometimes avoid being near that which we don't like or are uncomfortable with, it comes as no surprise that students want teachers to display nonverbal behaviors to show they care about the students, and proximity is one such behavior. Proximity honors learners by nonverbally saying to them that you see them and expect them to engage in the work. Proximity sends signals that you care.

Novelty

There are other strategies that lack a substantial body of research but help make the classroom an enjoyable place to learn. One of these is novelty. Our brains crave novelty (Jensen, 1998). Think back to times when you enjoyed the novelty someone offered you, whether it was a unique dish, new music, a special dance move, a lovely poem, or anything else that was new, unexpected, and fresh. Reflect on your personality and what makes you unique, and then share this with your students and in your classroom. Consider the following examples.

- Wear clothes that match the content of your lesson. For example, one day when delivering a lesson on the symbolism of evil in a poem, wear a sweater with a large serpent on it, or dress up as the characters in the historical period you are teaching or the novels students are reading.

- Offer a unique snack to students, such as kale chips or sweet potato chips. Open their eyes to new foods and unique tastes. You might share foods from the cultural backgrounds of the students in the class.

- If you have a collection, share it with your students. One teacher had an elephant collection, another collected baseball cards, and another did

scrapbooking. In addition to novelty, sharing your interests builds relationships with students.

- If you have students for a period such as homeroom with no set curriculum,
  teach them a skill; one teacher taught her entire fifth-grade class how to
  knit, and all students made scarves or hats for themselves.

- Grow a unique plant in your room, or house an exotic pet, if that is allowed.

- Share your unique passions, skills, loves, and activities with your students.
  Allow them to see and hear you as a unique human being. Survey them for
  their unique loves.

- Play a song when students enter the room that they associate with you and
  your room. Turning off the music can also be a signal to begin work.

- Hang things from the ceiling. One teacher hangs her student groups from
  the ceiling—not the real students, but the names of the students on individual stars.

- Create a different environment in your classroom if it belongs to you all
  day. Have a reading nook, a time-out corner for students who want to take
  a break (not punitive), a coffee or tea area (this may not be allowed in all
  schools, but it is done effectively in some high schools), a bookcase of read-
  and-return books, a futon for conversation, and so on.

The following examples show novelty related to lesson delivery.

- Have students read their papers out loud. Listeners have a rubric and can
  take notes.

- Teach from the back of the room.

- Take students on field trips.

- Bring in speakers tied to the content area.

- Take students outside of the school for a lesson that involves real-world materials, such as measuring the distance between the building and the street.

- Take students to different parts of the building for a lesson.

- Use the media center to teach students how to access information.

Humor

Although humor was not one of the most influential strategies, no one can deny
it makes a big difference in the classroom. When teachers use humor in a way that
lightens the tone of the classroom, it relaxes students and builds classroom community.
Teachers can use humor in the following ways. Remember, however, to avoid sarcasm.

- Read or tell a joke or a funny story to the class.
- Use self-deprecating humor.

- Use your body and make exaggerated gestures as you lecture.

- Dress up as a character to teach a lesson or do a book talk.

- Invite a colleague in to the class to share a story to demonstrate the collegiality among staff to students.

- Consider "laughter yoga," where one person begins laughing and keeps laughing; then others join in. Yes, it feels awkward at first, but it is good for stress relief.

Which of these strategies do you employ in your classroom?

Which strategies are you willing to try?

Conclusion

In this chapter, you read about many strategies to support your delivery of instruction. Some of these are research-based, high-yield strategies, such as goal setting, metacognition, academic vocabulary, and critical-thinking skills—and others, such as proximity, novelty, and humor have a more limited research base but are strategies learners enjoy. These strategies work across communities of color as well as with white students. All should be applied judiciously as you plan in collaborative conversations to design and implement the best instruction possible to meet standards. The next chapter provides numerous examples of culturally responsive, standards-based lessons being used by teachers in real classrooms.

CHAPTER 4

Engage Students in Standards-Based Lessons

The more the student becomes the teacher and the more the teacher becomes the learner, then the more successful are the outcomes.

—John Hattie

In planning the content of our instruction, Hattie (2012) asks us to consider the following question: "What knowledge and understanding should be taught?"(Kindle location 1390). Think about the discipline you teach. With this in mind, ask yourself these two additional questions from Hattie (2012): "What knowledge and understanding is important; and What knowledge and understanding is going to lead to the greatest cognitive understandings and gains?" (Kindle location 1390).

Too often our curricula are dictated by tests. We hope the Common Core paves the way for teachers to work collaboratively to create rigorous, engaging standards-based lessons that offer learners what is worth knowing. The lessons and units in this chapter provide opportunities for students to become the teacher and for the teacher to become the learner, leading to more successful outcomes. In these lessons, you find students engaged with the content and willing to teach it to others, and you find teachers engaged with the content and willing to learn from others, including their students. All are learners in the classroom. Hattie (2012) writes that we must teach students to *self-regulate* their learning. If we use differentiated instruction, as you find in the lessons in this chapter, students are working at levels at which they can attain the success criteria of the lessons. For differentiation to be successful, Hattie writes, "Teachers need to know, for each student, where that student begins and where he or she is in his or her journey towards meeting the success criteria of the lesson. Is that student a novice, somewhat capable, or proficient?" (Kindle location 2421). Once again, the better the teacher knows the students, the more the teacher can build in opportunities for learners to meet the standards.

As you read the lesson plans in this chapter, consider how the teacher builds in opportunities to assess gaps in knowledge or understanding and what strategies students need as they work toward their learning targets. Both teachers and students use 21st century skills to do this, and the lessons in this chapter incorporate those skills, such as the following.

- Creativity
- Critical thinking
- Problem solving
- Decision making and learning through choice
- Collaborative conversations with others and cooperative grouping
- Information and communications technology and information literacy
- Personal and social responsibility aligned with lesson content

In addition, because the teacher uses lessons that are interactive between teacher and students, they include culturally responsive strategies that build teacher-student relationships and offer multiple opportunities for student voice and visibility. These teachers model culturally responsive instruction, and they are culturally literate. They modify content for diverse student needs. They allow students to work at the highest levels of thinking and create and connect the learning to their own cultures and lives.

We begin with a writing lesson taught in a fourth-grade classroom—but it could be used at other grade levels because it has learners using their own bodies and minds to learn about themselves while practicing literacy skills. Next is a speaking unit for middle school students that, likewise, could be implemented at other levels. It supports learners finding and using their voices to become visible members of the classroom community. We include a lesson on critical thinking that, once again, can be taught with modification at many levels. We then move to a unit on slavery that confronts historical and cultural issues. Finally, we include a unit on the contemporary prison system that offers an opportunity for students to examine a current social justice issue.

These lessons and units were designed by teachers across the United States who work with learners in urban to suburban to rural areas to implement culturally responsive standards-based instruction that connects to and engages all learners. At the beginning of each lesson, you find the purpose of the lesson, the Common Core State Standards addressed in the lesson, the critical-thinking skills it uses, the enduring understanding and big questions, the outcomes of the lesson, and the culturally responsive instructional strategies used in the lesson. All of these elements are tied to the six-step framework.

Note that this chapter does not address how to map comprehensive units to the Common Core ELA standards. Consider using Kathy Tuchman Glass's (2012) book *Mapping Comprehensive Units to the ELA Common Core Standards, K–5* for this purpose. This chapter also doesn't address how to align your curriculum to the CCSS; you can find that topic in *Aligning Your Curriculum to the Common Core State Standards* by Joe Crawford (2012). There are numerous published books that provide resources for mapping and aligning the CCSS to curriculum. The purpose here is to provide examples of lessons from teachers who engage their learners and who are learners themselves. These lessons include the big ideas to guide student learning.

What are big ideas? Glass (2012) calls them essential understandings; Wiggins and McTighe (1998) call them enduring understandings or big ideas. Whatever you, your students, and your professional learning group choose to call them, they are the "conceptually based statements that teachers invent or borrow and use to design curriculum and instruction that emanate from standards" (Glass, 2012, p. 42). They are what we want learners to remember long after they've forgotten facts—facts that they can find in just seconds online. These big ideas support learners in making connections from one subject to another and, just as important, to their own lives.

Before looking at the lessons in the chapter, let's consider what Knight (2013) has to say about the planning process:

> Planning . . . involves a paradox of sorts. On the one hand, planning is essential, but on the other hand, when planning a unit or lesson, teachers must enter into the process aware that they may have to shift directions at some point if they are going to meet the needs of all their students and if they are going to exploit all the opportunities for learning that arise, like gifts, in the environment. (p. 34)

Sometimes, as teachers, we do all the planning work, but we leave students behind if we don't attend to them first as human beings and "exploit all the opportunities for learning that arise." Those opportunities for learning often arise at unpredictable times, and if we don't allow for teachable moments, then we may miss opportunities to reach the hearts and minds of all of our learners. We need to include the visibility and voice of each learner into even the most planned lesson we deliver. The following lessons engage students in higher-level thinking because they make them visible learners; at the same time, teachers participate with the students and become learners themselves.

Elementary Lesson: Using Mind and Body While Growing Literacy Skills

Marilyn Woodard is a veteran fourth-grade teacher at an award-winning elementary school. This lesson connects with every student in her class. After the students complete the lesson, they post their work on the walls of the classroom, showcasing the cultures of the students. The products of their lesson make it is easy to understand why all students enjoy this lesson.

The purpose of this lesson is certainly to teach the standards, but it goes beyond that. Marilyn uses this lesson to build community in her classroom. All the students are involved, and they share parts of themselves with their classmates and the teacher. The outcome of this lesson is that it builds relationships among the students because they learn about and discuss their commonalities to develop new and deeper bonds of community. The products of the lesson guarantee that it fulfills step 1 of the six-step framework by offering visibility and voice to each learner. Writing about their own bodies causes learners to open up and engage in ways they normally would not. The learners collaborate with each other as the staff does in step 2 of the six-step framework: collaborative conversations. In teaching the lesson, Marilyn uses step 3 of the framework when she embeds culturally responsive strategies and uses high-yield, research-based strategies such as goal setting and higher-level thinking skills, which are expressed through student writing. The lesson itself is step 4 of the framework. The lesson also includes step 5—feedback—which is discussed in more detail in the next chapter. Step 6—engaging in a cultural literacy journey—is also evident in the lesson as Marilyn and the students learn more about one another's cultures. This step is discussed in more detail in chapter 6, "Engage in a Cultural Literacy Journey" (page 155). Ultimately, this lesson incorporates all the steps of the six-step framework and supports students in becoming successful learners.

The inspiration for this lesson came from the book *The Best Part of Me* by Wendy Ewald (2002). This is a lesson Ewald used with students and teachers in the Durham, North Carolina, Public Schools. She also developed a program at the Center for Documentary Studies at Duke University to use photography as the beginning point in writing projects with children.

Common Core standards (NGA & CCSSO, 2010):

> **W.3.5**—*Write narratives to develop real or imagined experiences or events using effective technique, descriptive details, and clear event sequences. (p. 20)*

> **W.4.5**—*With guidance and support from peers and adults, develop and strengthen writing as needed by planning, revising, and editing. (p. 21)*

> **L.4.1**—*Demonstrate command of the conventions of standard English grammar and usage when writing or speaking. (p. 28)*

> **L.4.2**—*Demonstrate command of the conventions of standard English capitalization, punctuation, and spelling when writing. (p. 28)*

> **L.4.3**—*Use knowledge of language and its conventions when writing, speaking, reading, or listening. (p. 29)*

Anchor standards (NGA & CCSSO, 2010):

> **CCRA.W.3**—*Write narratives to develop real or imagined experiences or events using effective technique, well-chosen details, and well-structured event sequences. (p. 41)*

> **CCRA.W.5**—*Develop and strengthen writing as needed by planning, revising, editing, rewriting, or trying a new approach. (p. 41)*

> **CCRA.L.1**—*Demonstrate command of the conventions of standard English grammar and usage when writing or speaking. (p. 25)*

> **CCRA.L.2**—*Demonstrate command of the conventions of standard English capitalization, punctuation, and spelling when writing. (p. 25)*

> **CCRA.L.3**—*Apply knowledge of language to understand how language functions in different contexts, to make effective choices for meaning or style, and to comprehend more fully when reading or listening. (p. 25)*

Culturally responsive teaching strategies:

- **Connecting to the lives of the students**—*This lesson uses each student's own body parts as the object of the lesson.*

- **Honoring learners' voices and giving visibility to all**—*This lesson displays each student's picture on the classroom wall, providing visibility.*

- **Building teacher-student relationships**—*This lesson builds relationships through the individual teacher-student conferences built into the lesson.*

- **Fostering teacher expectations**—*This lesson fosters high expectations because there is an expectation that students will complete the activities.*

- **Giving feedback**—*This lesson offers ongoing feedback during the lesson.*

- **Setting goals**—*When students choose their body parts, they set a goal to create their project based on their choices.*

- **Using proximity**—*This lesson involves the teacher conferencing one-on-one with each student.*

- **Using higher-level thinking**—*This lesson focuses on creating, thus using higher-level thinking.*

- **Interacting with others**—*This lesson involves peer sharing throughout the process.*

- **Connecting to families**—*This lesson invites families into the classroom to observe final projects.*

- **Using movement**—*This lesson uses movement both inside and outside of the classroom.*

Strategies for differentiated instruction, RTI (response to intervention), and Tier 1 instruction:

- *Students have a choice of topic.*

- *Students work at their own pace to work toward a goal.*

- *Students have one-on-one interaction with the teacher during conferencing.*

- *Students get and give peer support with positive feedback.*

Big idea: *Opinions can be expressed in our writing.*

Enduring understanding: *Students will recognize that each of us has a "best part of our self," we can identify it, it is from our perception only, and that makes each of us unique.*

Day 1: *I (Marilyn) asked the children if they had ever thought about what physical part they liked best about themselves. I told them that I had been thinking about that very thing for myself. Before I told them what I thought was the best part of me, I wanted to read the book* The Best Part of Me *to them and let them think about what other children had chosen.*

I read the story slowly and showed them the pictures and writing of each child. They were mesmerized by what the children had chosen and why. We spent several minutes going back and choosing our favorite stories.

I told them that I thought the best part of me was my hair. The reason I chose that was because I love the color of my hair. It was the color of my mother's hair also. My hair has body and natural curl, so I have never messed with my hair much because it usually behaved on its own. It's just as well, because I'm not a whiz at fixing hair! People have often complimented me on my hair, because the color is different from most people's.

I had the students go back to their seats and start brainstorming in their journals about possible body parts they could write about. The next day we were going to choose the best part of ourselves to begin writing about in the lesson. We decided that we would sleep on it.

Day 2: *Today we reconvened, and I read the story to them again. We talked about reasons why the children in the book chose their best part.*

We checked out several reasons because we want to think about and write about our own opinion of what we think our best body part is.

The children went back to their journals and chose what their best body part was, and then began to brainstorm reasons for their choice.

I suggested they get really personal in their thinking. "Why are your blue eyes your best part? Did they come from your mother? Your grandmother? Is it because other people have told you that you have beautiful eyes? Is it because of the certain shade of blue they are?" I really wanted them to come up with their reasons why.

Day 3: *Today we took our body of work and came up with a catchy beginning to our story. Would it be: "I chose this _____ because . . ."? or "I like my _____, and this is why"? Strong beginnings set the tone of the piece. We talked over several possibilities.*

We also concentrated on appropriate ways to end. "Do we just state the beginning sentence again, or do we come up with something entirely different?" Again, we discussed several possibilities.

Day 4: *Today we put our pieces of work together and then shared them with a partner. Partners gave compliments and suggestions.*

During this time, we also did some revision work. We talked about sentence structure, punctuation, and grammar.

As students were working, I began pulling children aside to photograph that special part they were writing about. I asked for their suggestions and then offered up my own on the composition of the photos. They had very good ideas on their own! I took several poses so each student could choose what he or she liked best.

Day 5: *Taking everyone's pictures took a while, but we got it all done. I let each student choose which shot he or she liked best and then printed the photos out in black and white. The picture-taking and choosing was a really fun part of the project.*

To continue with the organic feel, I had my students write their stories instead of type them. Their handwriting added to the charm of the project.

Once the writing was finished, they glued their work and their pictures on to black construction paper.

This project had the students engaged from the beginning. They loved the idea of choosing the best part of themselves, naturally. They came up with incredible thoughts and sentiments. Their pride in their work was apparent. It didn't matter how smart they were, what color they were, or how attractive they were. Each person had that certain something to be proud about.

Sam (figure 4.1) said, "I liked letting others know what I can do with my hands. It made me feel proud." He learned that "I can do things that others can't do, and it doesn't matter what a person looks like, it makes you feel special." (M. Woodard, personal communication, March 27, 2013)

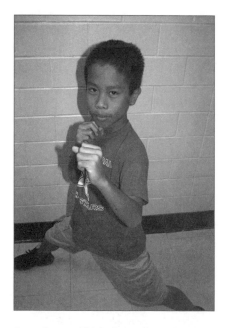

Figure 4.1: Sam showing off his hands.

Middle School: Developing Public Speaking Skills for the 21st Century

Middle school teacher Marcus Edwards offers students multiple ways of learning through multiple modes of expression. Technologically savvy, Marcus imbeds 21st century skills throughout his lessons to connect with learners and support them in becoming college and career ready.

In this lesson, Marcus teaches critical-thinking skills through interpretation and analysis of speeches, culminating with students giving a speech to seventh-grade students and receiving immediate feedback from the teacher. The purpose of this lesson is to teach social skills, public speaking, and the power of persuasion, and to build community in the classroom. Marcus pushes learners to confront their fears of public speaking and learn the power and force that being able to speak in public gives them, while using information literacy to support their research. The outcome of this lesson is a more cohesive group of middle school learners who have practiced the 21st century skills of collaboration, critical thinking, and problem solving. In this lesson, Marcus utilizes technology throughout to engage learners and strengthen their technological skills. Learners move through the six-step framework as they become individually visible and their voices are heard in their collaboration and during their speeches (step 1). They collaborate with classmates in round-table discussions (step 2). They are exposed to and use standards-based, high-yield strategies such as goal setting (step 3). They are immersed in a standards-based lesson (step 4). They give feedback and receive feedback from each other and the teacher (step 5—discussed in more depth in the next chapter), and they learn about the cultures of the others in their classroom (step 6—discussed in chapter 6, "Engage in a Cultural Literacy Journey," page 155).

In this lesson, students gain confidence, the ability to effectively deliver any material, resilience, and vigor. The unit can be taught to anyone of any age. I have used the public speaking piece in elementary and middle school.

Common Core standards (NGA & CCSSO, 2010):

SL.7.4—Present claims and findings, emphasizing salient points in a focused, coherent manner with pertinent description, facts, details, and examples: use appropriate eye contact, adequate volume, and clear pronunciation. (p. 49)

SL.7.5—Include multimedia components and visual displays in presentations to clarify claims and findings and emphasize salient points. (p. 49)

SL.7.6—Adapt speech to a variety of contexts and tasks, demonstrating command of formal English when indicated or appropriate. (p. 49)

Anchor standards (NGA & CCSSO, 2010):

CCRA.SL.4—Present information, findings, and supporting evidence such that listeners can follow the line of reasoning and the organization, development, and style are appropriate to task, purpose, and audience. (p. 42)

CCRA.SL.5—Make strategic use of digital media and visual displays of data to express information and enhance understanding of presentations. (p. 48)

CCRA.SL.6—Adapt speech to a variety of contexts and communication tasks, demonstrating command of formal English when indicated or appropriate. (p. 48)

Culturally responsive teaching strategies:

- **Connecting to students' lives**—*Students choose their own topics.*
- **Fostering teacher expectations**—*The teacher expects all students to participate.*
- **Building teacher-student relationships**—*The teacher works closely with students, fostering relationships.*
- **Building vocabulary**—*Students build vocabulary based on their topic of choice.*
- **Using study skills**—*Students learn how to prepare to give a speech.*
- **Setting goals**—*Students set goals for their speeches.*
- **Incorporating culturally relevant material**—*Before the students create their own speeches, they listen to several famous speeches given by diverse speakers from various cultures.*
- **Giving feedback**—*Each student receives immediate two-minute feedback from the teacher upon completion of his or her speech.*
- **Having collaborative conversations**—*Students collaborate as they plan and deliver speeches.*
- **Learning culturally relevant social skills**—*Students learn skills for influencing others through communication.*

Strategies for differentiated instruction, RTI, and Tier 1 instruction:

- *Students choose their topic of study.*
- *The teacher works one-on-one with students through planning, delivery, and immediate feedback.*

- *Students collaborate and share with their peers.*
- *Students work at their own pace.*

Big idea: *Social skills are learned, refined, and highly useful in life.*

Enduring understanding: *Speaking is a way to influence others.*

I (Marcus) created the lesson to expose middle school students to the power of social skills and presenting oneself with professional charisma and confidence. As we go through life, we develop a skill set to communicate with one another. Some develop great skills through experiences with family, educators, and peers—whereas others do not have the opportunity to develop their social skills. In the professional world, presenting information and communicating effectively is a learned skill that allows people to advance in their professions. I stress the importance of these learned and practiced social skills.

Creating this experience involves setting an emotional tone. Students look to you, as a teacher, first as a performer—show off your skills, and make learning a memorable experience. Express to students that in the activity they will deliver a speech that is powerful, emotional, and relevant.

Phase 1: *After you have grasped the student's attention, let them express interest and focus on a topic with a tool such as TodaysMeet (https://todaysmeet.com) or Padlet (https://padlet.com), which are both web 2.0 tools that allow students to share ideas in real time. Project student posts on a screen, and give them the opportunity to elaborate on their posts.*

Phase 2: *Allow students to search for, watch, listen to, and read great speeches. Encourage them to analyze the speeches and express their thoughts on the components of great speeches. Allow groups to combine their thoughts and create worlds, videos, or animated explanations. Create a website, if you don't already have one, that includes links to speeches in a variety of forms. A website allows your students to access to the amazing things you are doing in class. Use it to post explanation videos, class discussions, and links to web 2.0 tools for creating content. (See https://wiki.rockwallisd.org/groups /medwards for Marcus's website.) You can create a website from many free sites. Test drive them, and see which format is the best fit. One great source for viewing master speakers is www.TED.com; there are a* *variety of topics you can select from. Make sure to preview any speeches you choose or link to for suitability, so there are no surprises.*

Phase 3: *In this phase of the lesson, students will be focused on learning the skill set necessary for mastering public speaking. Provide them with guides for brainstorming, speech structure, dos and don'ts, and mastering the delivery of the speech. Create a rubric for this phase. A rubric allows the students the opportunity to guide their learning. This rubric or guide can be simple or complex. I have found that communicating with students properly will eliminate any confusion.*

Once students learn about public speaking and understand its formalities, they share their mastery of the skill set needed to be a great public speaker. Direct students by asking, "How can you show me you have mastered the skill set?" This opens up the doors for student creativity. Also address audience etiquette, such as by teaching and practicing clapping.

Phase 4: *In this final phase, students use their fine-tuned skill sets to create a masterpiece of public speaking: the speech. They construct a speech that allows them to express their interest, position, or ideas using the structure they have learned. Encourage students to practice performing their speeches at home for family or friends. When it comes time for the speeches, it is crucial to provide a new setting, such as the cafeteria or theatre. Search the building for props, a public address system, or make a pretend microphone. This will elevate the student's drive to perform and to master this skill and embrace the experience. Once the students perform, praise them, critique them, and ultimately encourage them to continue their public speaking. In my class, I allow the students the opportunity to receive feedback from the students as well as myself. The student feedback is limited to eye contact, volume, and of course, all the positives.*

This experience helps students understand that public speaking is a learned skill—not a skill people are born with. They will face a fear and overcome it and, ultimately, gain a skill that will allow them to rapidly progress in other endeavors. One student commented, "After doing this activity, I have been able to conquer my fears and talk to kids in other classes." (M. Edwards, personal communication, April 7, 2013)

As evidenced in the lesson, Marcus teaches students valuable lessons within his lessons. He is teaching literacy skills, social skills, and character education, all while practicing differentiation and using culturally responsive strategies within a standards-based lesson.

High School: Teaching Critical-Thinking Skills Through Architecture

Christina Steffen is the director of academic services at Central Methodist University. Her doctoral research is on critical thinking. A former art teacher, she has taught in several settings: public schools, online classes, private universities, and a university educating only women in the Middle East. In the following unit, she demonstrates how you can infuse critical thinking into a unit on art that can be taught across grade levels. In chapter 3 (pages 75–77), she discussed a lesson teachers were learning in her class in Saudi Arabia. In the lesson in this chapter, she displays her love of art by merging architecture with the lesson to teach critical-thinking skills and provide writing extensions for students. The lesson can be adapted to different grade levels.

In this lesson, Christina's purpose is to teach and use critical-thinking skills to meet several of the Common Core State Standards. Students practice comparing and contrasting each day of the lesson, create mind maps, and write arguments to support their claims, using skills of analysis substantiated by research. This lesson demonstrates how one can teach traditional material with an emphasis on the critical-thinking skills students need to be college and career ready. The outcomes of this lesson include a class of learners who feel more a part of a community after having collaborated with each other, having done self-assessment and peer assessment, having used higher-level thinking to arrive at the big questions and essential understandings of the lesson, and having used reflection as a tool to further their learning. Step 1 and step 2 of the framework are evident in the projects the students create and in their collaboration. No one is invisible. Step 3 is evident in the strategies Christina employs to teach the lesson, including higher-level critical-thinking skills, technology, creativity through art, mind maps, and comparing and contrasting. Step 4 is Christina teaching the lesson to the standards. Step 5, covered in the next chapter, is providing feedback to the students based on their work, and step 6, covered in chapter 6 "Engage in a Cultural Literacy Journey" (page 155), is learning from each other, honoring the different cultural perspectives of each learner. Some parts of the lesson are adapted from Robert J. Swartz and Sandra Parks's (1994) book *Infusing the Teaching of Critical and Creative Thinking Into Content Instruction*.

Common Core standards (NGA & CCSSO, 2010):

> **W.9–10.1**—*Write arguments to support claims in an analysis of substantive topics or texts, using valid reasoning and relevant and sufficient evidence. (p. 45)*

> **W.9–10.5**—*Develop and strengthen writing as needed by planning, revising, editing, rewriting, or trying a new approach, focusing on addressing what is most significant for a specific purpose and audience. (p. 46)*

> **W.9–10.6**—*Use technology, including the Internet to produce, publish, and update individual or shared writing products, taking advantage of technology's capacity to link to other information and to display information flexibly and dynamically. (p. 46)*

> **L.9–10.4**—*Determine or clarify the meaning of unknown and multiple-meaning words and phrases based on grades 9–10 reading and content, choosing flexibly from a range of strategies. (p.55)*

> **L.9–10.6**—*Acquire and use accurately general academic and domain-specific words and phrases, sufficient for reading, writing, speaking, and listening at the college and career readiness level; demonstrate independence in gathering vocabulary knowledge when considering a word or phrase important to comprehension or expression. (p. 55)*

Anchor standards (NGA & CCSSO, 2010):

> **CCRA.W.1**—*Write arguments to support claims in an analysis of substantive topics or texts, using valid reasoning and relevant and sufficient evidence. (p. 41)*

> **CCRA.W.5**—*Develop and strengthen writing as needed by planning, revising, editing, rewriting, or trying a new approach. (p. 41)*

> **CCRA.W.6**—*Use technology, including the Internet, to produce and publish writing and to interact and collaborate with others. (p. 41)*

> **CCRA.L.4**—*Determine or clarify the meaning of unknown and multiple-meaning words and phrases by using context clues, analyzing meaningful word parts, and consulting general and specialized reference materials, as appropriate. (p. 51)*

> **CCRA.L.6**—*Acquire and use accurately a range of general academic and domain-specific words and phrases sufficient for reading, writing,*

speaking, and listening at the college and career readiness level; demonstrate independence in gathering vocabulary knowledge when considering a word or phrase important to comprehension or expression. (p. 51)

Culturally responsive teaching strategies:

- **Using cooperative groups**—*Students work in groups to complete the lesson.*

- **Honoring learners' voices**—*Learners share their voices within the group.*

- **Making work visible**—*Students post their work on the wall.*

- **Giving feedback**—*The teacher gives feedback throughout the lesson, and students give feedback to each other.*

- **Learning vocabulary**—*Students learn content-specific vocabulary.*

- **Building teacher expectations**—*The teacher expects all students to participate.*

Strategies for differentiated instruction, RTI, and Tier 1 instruction:

- *Students have choice in their designs.*

- *Students review work with their peers and share throughout the process.*

- *Students are learning in multiple modalities.*

Big idea: *Architecture conveys the ideals held by a society as well as being a structure for use by that society.*

Enduring understanding: *Students will recognize that members of a society express their ideals through the things they create and build.*

As students enter the classroom, I (Christina) show them a model or picture of the Parthenon and another government building, such as a courthouse or post office. I ask students to write down everything they see in the model or picture of both structures.

I begin the lesson by asking students what they saw in the two models or pictures. Have they ever seen these buildings before? Where? I ask students who might not be familiar with ancient Greek architecture what the buildings represent. Is there a message they convey? I then ask students what forms they see and what they think the function might be.

I then divide the class into groups and assign each group a part of the Parthenon, such as the columns, the steps, the roof, and so on. I provide pictures of the Parthenon or project an image on the SMART Board.

Each group then researches its part. Feedback can come at this point as the teacher observes each group and students' conversations about each part. Use the following questions to guide the students' research and thinking:

- *What is the purpose or function of the part?*

- *What is the relationship or connection between the part of the Parthenon and the whole (the entire structure)? Here is where students can interpret, discuss, explain, compare, contrast, analyze, and synthesize all the information by writing about it. Require students to reflect on their thinking and not make just one or two statements.*

- *If the part were missing, what would happen to the Parthenon (the structure or building)? How would it change the message, symbolism, and so on?*

- *Can you describe your thinking as you went through this process? What made you decide on a particular part? Why did you choose it? How did you determine what might happen if the part were missing? How did you determine the relationship of the part to the whole structure?*

Next, each group exchanges its part with another group and teaches the group about its part. Repeat this step depending on size of class. Thus, groups learn about every part and its function.

The next step in the lesson is to compare and contrast with mind mapping. Mind maps organize information and visually guide thinking. You can display examples of mind maps on a SMART Board to show students the endless possibilities. Mind maps can be small, the size of notebook paper, or in some cases (my students mind mapped an entire chapter in their textbook, thirty pages) measured in feet! In addition, mind maps can be created using all kinds of materials. I've used yarn, buttons, ribbon, pictures, craft material shapes, and numbers.

If students have not had instructions comparing and contrasting, model a lesson. You may use a Venn diagram to show students how to compare and contrast two things.

Assign each group a temple in ancient Greece, such as the Temple of the Maidens, Temple of Zeus, Temple of Athena, and so on, or a modern building reflective of Greek architectural elements, such as the Second Bank of the United States.

Each group creates a mind map that demonstrates all the architectural elements of its building. (You can decide on the total number of elements.) For younger groups, you might model this part using a different building. Give feedback through observation.

Upon completion of the mind map, each group presents its research to the class and displays its work by hanging it up in the classroom. This is very important, because students can see their learning on a daily basis and use their mind maps for transferring learning.

After students have organized their information using mind maps, they can begin finding similarities and differences between the ancient Greek temple and a modern structure or building. Students can consider different elements, location of the temple or building, and so on. For example, How are the columns on the temple the same or different than the modern building? Where is the temple compared to the location of the modern building?

Students can work in groups or individually as all the information needed is displayed on the mind maps. Students may begin the process by bulleting the similarities and differences. Feedback here might come by requiring the students to have at least five similarities or differences depending on the flow of the lesson.

Finally, ask students to write one powerful statement or conclusion about the similarities and differences. Students tend to write, "There are many similarities and differences between the temple of _____ and the _____."

(C. Steffen, personal communication, April 17, 2013)

Visit **go.solution-tree.com/instruction** to find extension activities for teaching critical-thinking strategies through architecture.

Art and architecture reflect the cultures of those who create it, and we learn much about a culture through observing its art and architecture. Christina's lesson shows students how cultures create objects that reflect their values. In the next lesson, high school teacher Nancy Saguto shows how the institution of slavery influenced the culture of the United States not only in past centuries but also in the present one.

Cultural Literacy: Discovering How the Past Affects the Present

Nancy Saguto is a literacy coach and reading specialist at a high school. In the past, she taught in a school for homeless children, in homeless shelters, and in elementary, middle, and high schools where she taught many homeless students and undocumented students. Because Nancy was teaching in a high-poverty high school—where the majority of the students were from communities of color, Hispanic and African American, primarily—she needed to know as much as possible about the histories of these cultural groups and how these histories affected their families today. The purpose of the lesson she shares here was to educate her students on how the past affects the present and the future, while practicing the skills dictated by the CCSS. In a course called "Coming to America," Nancy presented a unit based on groups forced to immigrate to this country. Knowing the volatility of such a topic, Nancy was careful about including activities in which learners could reflect, share, vent, and display their grief through writing and ceremony. This lesson, designed for eleventh-grade students, used the six-step framework in the following ways: Step 1 involved each student taking part in the discussions, creating poems, and doing image gathering to display in the classroom. Throughout the lesson, learners discuss and reflect with each other (step 2). Step 3 includes many differentiated instructional strategies and higher-level strategies as the learners make decisions about their own learning, create various kinds of poetry, write at higher levels, and incorporate movement and other strategies for their learning. Step 4 is the lesson, a multisensory lesson that incorporates technology, critical thinking, and problem solving in response to the big questions asked by the learners and ties the material to the present day by discussing things such as post-traumatic stress experienced by slaves and the residual results of slavery that permeate communities of color today. Step 5 (covered in the next chapter) includes the responses learners offer each other throughout the lesson as well as the self-assessment and feedback from the teacher. Finally, this lesson is a superb example of step 6 (chapter 6, "Engage in a Cultural Literacy Journey," page 155) in that the lesson evolved from the teacher's quest to learn more about what she did not know she didn't know and then broadened that into a lesson for her students, offering them an opportunity to learn about the cultural experiences of others.

If you want to engage learners, do what Nancy does: investigate the provocative realities of your students' lives. The outcomes of this lesson include the further building of a classroom community that investigates difficult topics together in the process of practicing skills dictated by the CCSS.

Common Core standards (NGA & CCSSO, 2010):

> **RL.11–12.1**—*Cite strong and thorough textual evidence to support analysis of what the text says explicitly as well as inferences drawn from the text, including determining where the text leaves matters uncertain. (p. 38)*

> **RL.11–12.4**—*Determine the meaning of words and phrases as they are used in the text, including figurative and connotative meanings; analyze the cumulative impact of specific word choices on meaning and tone. (p. 38)*

> **RI.11–12.9**—*Analyze seventeenth-, eighteenth-, and nineteenth-century foundational U.S. documents of historical and literary significance (including The Declaration of Independence, the Preamble to the Constitution, the Bill of Rights, and Lincoln's Second Inaugural Address) for their themes, purposes, and rhetorical features. (p. 40)*

> **W.11–12.6**—*Use technology, including the Internet, to produce, publish, and update individual or shared writing products in response to ongoing feedback, including new arguments or information. (p. 46)*

> **W.11–12.4**—*Produce clear and coherent writing in which the development, organization, and style are appropriate to task, purpose, and audience. (p. 46)*

Anchor standards (NGA & CCSSO, 2010):

> **CCRA.R.1**—*Read closely to determine what the text says explicitly and to make logical inferences from it; cite specific textual evidence when writing or speaking to support conclusions drawn from the text. (p. 60)*

> **CCRA.R.4**—*Interpret words and phrases as they are used in a text including determining technical, connotative, and figurative meanings, and analyze how specific word choices shape meaning or tone. (p. 60)*

> **CCRA.R.10**—*Read and comprehend complex literary and informational texts independently and proficiently. (p. 60)*

> **CCRA.W.4**—*Produce clear and coherent writing in which the development, organization, and style are appropriate to task, purpose, and audience. (p. 41)*

CCRA.W.6—*Use technology, including the Internet, to produce and publish writing and to interact and collaborate with others. (p. 41)*

Culturally responsive teaching strategies:

- *Using cooperative groups*—*Learners work in groups.*
- *Building teacher expectations*—*The teacher expects all students to participate.*
- *Using technology*—*Learners use technology for research and viewing videos on the topic.*
- *Building vocabulary*—*Learners acquire content-specific words.*
- *Connecting content to students' interests*—*The topic is relevant to all students because it is a part of U.S. history, and perhaps especially relevant to communities of color.*

Strategies for differentiated instruction, RTI, and Tier 1 instruction:

- *Students have choice of reading materials.*
- *Students decide how to focus on a topic.*
- *Learners choose texts based on their interest and reading levels.*
- *Learners share and process together with peer review.*

Big idea: *We need to learn our history in order not to repeat the atrocities of our past.*

Enduring understanding: *Education empowers people to resist being enslaved.*

How little I (Nancy) know about history is often a source of regret for me. It was only as an adult I realized how poorly I was taught in school—and more dishearteningly, how much I wasn't taught even though I went to fine schools. One area I was woefully ill-informed about was slavery in America. Fortunately, I was a participant in the Missouri Humanities Project—an extended professional development initiative that allowed me to examine many aspects of teaching, learning, and cultural literacy. During one year, part of the focus of our study was slavery in America, and one of our presenters was a professor from a local university.

Part of our study of slavery focused on people's perceptions of who the slaves were. Professor Smith's insights were startling in some ways, especially when he talked about the number of women and children who were brought here on ships. He pointed out that most people's picture of a slave is one of a young, strong man in chains. We learned about why certain images are not present in our perceptions of slavery and also about the idea of slave resistance. For the most part, knowledge about slave resistance is not a part of history, and we looked at the reasons for this. After these sessions, I brought these ideas back to my classroom and studied them with my students.

In one of my classes, we considered these ideas in relationship to the Narrative of the Life of Frederick Douglass *(1987) and the slave narratives we were reading. We talked at length about why the slaves' stories were not told until the time the narratives were recorded in the 1930s. We compared several of the slave experiences with that of Douglass. When comparing Douglass with other slaves, the students discovered what they thought was the defining element in Douglass's ability to resist his oppressors: the fact that Douglass could read and write.*

We considered why slaves were kept from an education and why they experienced many other devastating conditions of a slave's life. After the students read and responded to several narratives, they began to generate questions about slaves and slavery that had not yet been answered to their satisfaction. I typed up all of their questions and then cut them apart into strips. I then gave a set of question strips to each group of students to sort, categorize, and label. This was a powerful exercise. Questions centered around issues such as the following.

- *Why didn't the slaves resist?*
- *Did the slaves experience post-traumatic stress disorder?*
- *Did the slaves lose hope forever?*
- *Why didn't more people help them out?*

The students then researched answers and presented their findings back to the class. They uncovered new information, as well as many more questions.

At the end of our study, I had the students choose the strips with questions that most spoke to them and had them glue these strips on a piece of paper. They then wrote a free-write response to each question. Finally, they used these responses to write a poem. We called them "strip poetry." Their poems were powerful. The students felt an urgency about communicating the horrors they had learned about, almost as a tribute to the people who had suffered so catastrophically.

Different classes have responded differently to the slavery study; different aspects of the study have resonated with them. Some of the aspects they have been drawn to include:

- *The readings and poetry*

- *The Underground Railroad and its heroes*

- *Racism*

- *Historical events and places*

- *Abolitionists*

- *Remnants of slavery in today's culture*

- *Modern-day slavery*

- *The effect of slavery on modern-day Africa*

- *Post-traumatic stress disorder*

- *Slave reparations*

- *Rewriting textbooks to tell a more complete history of slavery in America*

A study like this easily accommodates a wide range of interests, talents, and abilities and is also easily differentiated for instruction. Throughout the unit, there is variety in the types of readings, books to read, and writings, and students also have a choice about what to focus on. Students research their own questions and also direct the focus of the unit. The class is very collaborative in nature, and most of the work is done in small groups. Following are some of the components of the slavery study.

KWL Chart

I usually begin with each student filling out a hybrid version of a KWL (know, want to know, learned) chart. I give students plenty of time, so they can think at length about the topic. After they fill out their individual charts, I have the class work together to create a class KWL that includes everyone's responses. I have these made into a big poster that is displayed throughout the unit as a reference to guide our study. Figure 4.2 shows a sample KWL chart.

Vocabulary

Throughout the unit, students keep track of words they encounter that will express the different aspects of slavery. In particular, I have them collect words and images from the Frederick Douglass memoir. We keep a large piece of chart paper on the wall so that students can add their words to it. One other activity I do is a lesson on degrees of word meanings. On a seven-line handout, I have students begin the activity by putting the word annoyed on the bottom line. Next to the word, the

What I Think I Know for Sure About This Topic	What I Think I Know but Am Not Sure About This Topic	What I Would Like to Learn About This Topic	Connections Between This Topic and Other Things I Know
Slavery has existed for thousands of years. Without slavery, this country probably would not have survived. If it did survive, it would be very different than it is now. Slavery had long-lasting consequences for both the slaves and the slave owners. Slavery devastated a large part of the population. We did not know the truth about slavery until fairly recently. Slave owners controlled what people knew about slaves and slavery. Slavery turns slave owners into animals. There were remarkable stories about slaves that we still don't know. The effects of slavery are still present in society today.	Some slaves were treated better than others. There were different situations for slaves—some could buy themselves. Freed slaves bought Native Americans as slaves. There were slaves in the North. The slaves didn't get to tell their own story, so people thought they liked being slaves.	Who were the first slaves in the world? How did slavery start? Was there slavery in the North or not? Can a culture ever recover from the effects of slavery? Can slavery convince the slaves that they are inferior? How did Christians reconcile their religion with owning slaves? What would I have done if I were a slave? What kept the slaves from killing themselves? What is denial? How come we don't know about how brave the slaves were? Could the slaves buy themselves?	Sex slaves Prison Prisoners of war Cults Jim Crow laws Underground Railroad Civil rights Civil War Abolitionists Racism Sweatshops The Holocaust

Figure 4.2: Sample KWL chart for slavery unit.

students give a definition in their own words. Finally, on the line, they describe a situation in which someone would be annoyed. Next, on the line at the top, students confer to come up with a word that would be the extreme version of annoyed. *For example, they might choose* enraged. *Again, they write a definition of* enraged *in their own words, and finally describe a situation in which someone might be enraged. Next, students work to complete the chart, finding words that gradually increase in intensity from* annoyed *to* enraged. *This exercise helps students focus on being specific and refined in their word choice. In the end, we are trying to build a word bank to use when we write the poetry later in the unit. Students also keep track of character traits they encounter in their many readings, and these are also recorded on chart paper.*

Quote and Image Gathering

Throughout the study, students collect quotes and images they encounter that strike them as memorable. They record these items for all to see. In the end, students choose quotes to illustrate in some way and then display them.

Poetry

Slavery and poetry are a natural pairing because poetry can so well express the complexity of emotions and ideas associated with the horrors of slavery. Throughout the unit, we read several poems about slavery including Sympathy *and* We Wear the Mask *by Paul Laurence Dunbar (Braxton, 1993) and* Frederick Douglass *(Hayden, 1966). We also create our own poems. In addition to the strip poetry described earlier, we write haiku, cinquains, and five-line poems. Using words from the word wall, students are quite successful when creating the haiku and cinquains.*

Readings and Writing

There are numerous readings you can include for this study in addition to poetry. Nonfiction readings include the slave narratives (Taylor, 2007), advice about how to read the slave narratives, primary sources, essays about modern slavery, and post-traumatic stress disorder. Fiction readings include novels students can choose to read in small groups, such as Chains *(Anderson, 2005),* Forge *(Anderson, 2012),* Copper Sun *(Draper, 2006), and* 47 *(Mosley, 2006). During the lesson, students*

create several poems. While reading the Frederick Douglass memoir,
students respond in writing to several prompts and also complete a
double-entry journal for the Douglass reading (see figure 4.3 for an
example), the novels, and the slave narratives.

Directions: Choose three passages from the text that strike you in some way—for their meaning, the pictures they stimulate in your mind, the ideas you have about the passage, and the associations or the feelings they generate. Copy each passage in the left column. In the right column, write your response to each passage. (The right column should be full of your writing.)

Passages From the Text	Response to the Passage
"Mr. Covey succeeded in breaking me. I was broken in body, soul, and spirit. My natural elasticity was crushed, my intellect languished, the disposition to read departed, the cheerful spark that lingered about my eye died; the dark night of slavery closed in upon me; and behold a man transformed into a brute!" (p. 73)	I can't believe this! I thought he would give up at different places, but now I don't want him to lose his heart and give up. I was scared for him that he wouldn't have his spirit after this happened. I don't know how he did survive.
"You are loosed from your moorings, and are free; I am fast in my chains, and am a slave! You move merrily before the gentle gale, and I sadly before the bloody whip! You are freedom's swift-winged angels, that fly round the world; I am confined in bands of iron! O that I were free!" (p. 73)	This is one of the most powerful and devastating parts of the narrative. You can just feel how helpless Douglass is and how completely caught like an animal. He imagines what freedom would feel like and constantly compares that to his suffering. My favorite description is where he compares the boats to "freedom's swift-winged angels."
"You have seen how a man was made a slave; you shall see how a slave was made a man." (p. 75)	He fought Mr. Covey in the barn. He was choking Covey and beat him. He decided to fight Covey, and when he won, he said he would never let another man beat or whip him without a fight. He would defend himself no matter what. He said that Covey had turned him into a brute, but now he was turned back into a man because he risked his life to beat Covey.

Source: Douglass, 1987.

Figure 4.3: Sample double-entry journal response.

Expanding the Study

Over a period of three years, what began as a small unit ended up as a semester-long project that could easily be expanded to a year-long study. Student response to the study of slavery was stunning. They took control of the investigation, continually asked and researched more questions, followed leads and made connections—and in the end, the students decided they needed to honor the slaves for their bravery and suffering by creating a truly inspiring memorial wall with their own writings, poetry, and artwork displayed in an area they surrounded with a string of tiny white lights. They planned a reception for the completion of the memorial wall and invited family, friends, and staff members to attend. They created their own program, made presentations about things they had discovered, and read their poetry aloud. They even had a soundtrack of very moving music they created including protest songs and spirituals playing in the background. It was one of the most moving events I have ever attended. No one who attended will ever forget it, and the students felt they truly had honored the slaves in a very lovely manner.

My admiration for my students was high after all they accomplished. As part of their final exam, I asked the students to respond to at least three of the following questions:

- *In your opinion, why is it important for people, in general, to know about what the slaves went through in America?*

- *What have you learned from our study of slavery that has changed you or your thinking in some way?*

- *For you, what are the most important big ideas you will take away from our study of slavery?*

- *What advice do you think slaves would have for teenagers in America today?*

- *What life lessons have you learned that you will take with you from this study?*

Students' writing in response to these questions showed me how truly rich their learning had been. They clearly explained how they had been changed and how important the life lessons they learned were to them. Their insights were thoughtful and profound. They all felt they were better people because of what they had experienced.

The topic of slavery is uncomfortable. Studying this atrocity may cause students to feel many emotions such as anger, sadness, grief, depression, and despair. Nancy supports her students in exposing their grief through the exercises in the unit, but if you choose to teach this unit, you may want to talk with your school counselor or social worker and ask for suggestions for supporting learners as they encounter and learn about this part of our collective history.

Visit **go.solution-tree.com/instruction** to find a list of additional resources for the slavery unit, including books, videos, images, and slave memorials.

Mary Kim Schreck created the next lesson for high school students. Understanding the prison crisis the United States is now experiencing, Mary Kim believed others needed to know what they didn't know they didn't know about the crisis. Focusing on the topic using text sets, Mary Kim creates a riveting lesson sure to engage even the most disinterested older student. Once again, during this lesson, students becomes teachers of their own learning, and teacher Mary Kim learns right along with her students as she studies the impact of her own teaching.

Focusing on a Topic With Text Sets

Text sets, a combination of different materials focused on a topic, have been in teachers' repertoires for decades. For example, we used lyrics from Simon and Garfunkel's songs to teach figurative language. We used newspapers to supplement the literature we were teaching. We used political cartoons and art from every source we could cull—student art, graffiti, the masters. Even though this was before videos and websites, we did have radio, television, newspapers, and books of poetry—and from these, we created text sets. Consequently, the idea of using a combination of materials is not new, but the added rigor of the CCSS dictates we enhance the content with additional resources, thus text sets. You can even find a workshop on using text sets at Annenberg Learner (www.learner.org/workshops/tml/workshop4 /teaching.html).

In *Overcoming Textbook Fatigue: 21st Century Tools to Revitalize Teaching and Learning*, ReLeah Cossett Lent (2012) includes several suggestions for creating text sets with websites to support the work. The last lesson, created by Nancy Saguto, also was an example of a text sets lesson in that she used multiple texts and different materials as resources for the lesson. Following is another text set from Mary Kim Schreck that she created on the prison system in the United States, a topic of interest to both of us.

This lesson focuses on a major issue in the United States, the prison system, one I learned something about when I taught in a maximum security prison for seven semesters. The common denominator with the prisoners in my classes—usually about half men of color and half white men—was the fact that they grew up in poverty. The purpose of Mary Kim's lesson is to immerse learners in a controversial topic that engages them and informs them about a major challenge faced in the United States today. Mary Kim's lesson has learners ask hard questions about the incarceration system we employ and to generate solutions to this problem. In this lesson, step 1 of the framework is apparent as learners generate questions, discuss with each other, and honor each other's voice and opinions. Step 2 is the collaboration the group members employ as they create the text sets along with the teacher and reflect on the collection. Step 3 is the myriad of strategies Mary Kim uses with her learners to create this learning experience. They write, use technology, create, and generate—all based on a topic that engages them in a personal way. Step 4 is the lesson. Step 5 (discussed in chapter 5, "Use Feedback to Self-Assess Learning," page 121) is the continual feedback they receive and give to peers along with their self-reflection and feedback from the teacher. Step 6 (discussed in chapter 6, "Engage in a Cultural Literacy Journey," page 155) is the opportunity this lesson gives them to learn about the experiences of those incarcerated individuals who make up an alarming percentage of our population, especially when compared to other industrialized nations. This is a controversial topic that leads learners to new insights about their own cultures and the cultures of others. The outcome is that learners become more closely affiliated as classmates as they interrogate a difficult topic and work to find solutions for the future. Other outcomes include practicing the skills demanded by the CCSS.

Common Core standards (NGA & CCSSO, 2010):

RI.11–12.1—Cite strong and thorough textual evidence to support analysis of what the text says explicitly as well as inferences drawn from the text, including determining where the text leaves matters uncertain. (p. 38)

RI.11–12.7—Integrate and evaluate multiple sources of information presented in different media or formats. (p. 62)

W.11–12.4—Produce clear and coherent writing in which the development, organization, and style are appropriate to task, purpose, and audience. (p. 46)

W.11–12.9—*Draw evidence from literary or informational texts to support analysis, reflection, and research. (p. 47)*

SL.11–12.1—*Initiate and participate effectively in a range of collaborative discussions. (p. 50)*

SL.11–12.4—*Present information, findings, and supporting evidence, conveying a clear and distinct perspective, such that listeners can follow the line of reasoning, alternative or opposing perspectives are addressed, and the organization, development, substance, and style are appropriate to purpose, audience, and a range of formal and informal tasks. (p. 50)*

L.11–12.3—*Apply knowledge of language to understand how language functions in different contexts, to make effective choices for meaning or style, and to comprehend more fully when reading or listening. (p. 54)*

Anchor standards (NGA & CCSSO, 2010):

CCRA.R.1—*Read closely to determine what the text says explicitly and to make logical inferences from it; cite specific textual evidence when writing or speaking to support conclusions drawn from the text. (p. 60)*

CCRA.R.7—*Integrate and evaluate content presented in diverse formats and media, including visually and quantitatively, as well as in words. (p. 60)*

CCRA.W.4—*Produce clear and coherent writing in which the development, organization, and style are appropriate to task, purpose, and audience. (p. 41)*

CCRA.W.9—*Draw evidence from literary or informational texts to support analysis, reflection, and research. (p. 41)*

CCRA.SL.1—*Prepare for and participate effectively in a range of conversations and collaborations with diverse partners, building on others' ideas and expressing their own clearly and persuasively. (p. 48)*

CCRA.SL.4—*Present information, findings, and supporting evidence such that listeners can follow the line of reasoning and the organization, development, and style are appropriate to task, purpose, and audience. (p. 48)*

CCRA.L.3—*Apply knowledge of language to understand how language functions in different contexts, to make effective choices for meaning or style, and to comprehend more fully when reading or listening. (p. 51)*

Culturally responsive teaching strategies:

- *Students work together and individually.*
- *Building in movement, getting close to students (proximity), and offering lessons in multiple modalities increases student interest and investment in the lessons.*

Strategies for differentiated instruction, RTI, and Tier 1 instruction:

- *Learners are given choice in the question they investigate.*
- *Learners use technology to work at their own levels.*
- *Learners work in groups with peers to share and process.*
- *Learners work at their own pace.*

Big idea: *Issues of law and order are complex, and their truths are seldom distinguishable on the surface.*

Enduring understanding: *Well-meaning institutions often evolve into organizations whose main purpose is to sustain their own existence.*

If I (Mary Kim) was starting a lesson on the Aztecs and Mayans and studying the idea of jobs in the cultures, I could begin the unit with questions about how students think the Aztecs and Mayans spent their time. We typically begin a lesson or unit with older students by initiating questions that might guide us in our exploration. Most student-driven classrooms and project-based learning situations are like this. They start with a common set of questions but quickly move toward questions brought up by the students themselves that will serve to propel their interests into and through the study of the topic. Teachers moving into this form of instruction often experience a kind of tension between wanting to run the show themselves and wanting to allow the students more input into their ownership of the learning.

A good way to ease into this letting go of the reins would be for the class to brainstorm all possible questions that could arise concerning the topic to be investigated and for the group to come to a consensus on what the central questions should be that everyone will consider. This might be any number—three to six good questions, perhaps. With whole-class agreement, we now can begin our work.

The Common Core Writing standards emphasize the ability to write logical arguments based on substantive claims: reasoning and relevant evidence. The Common Core Reading standards emphasize the need to analyze how two or more texts address similar themes or topics in order to build knowledge. The Common Core literacy standards as aptly interpreted by EngageNY, a collaborative platform for teachers in New York, is a complement to the content standards of all other areas to ensure that teachers create carefully structured situations that allow students to solve problems independently and encourage students to draw on their abilities to discover answers by themselves, rather than rely on adults to supply the facts (EngageNY, n.d.).

Let's see how this might look using the topic of incarceration. Questions students might identify for this topic might include the following:

- Have we always had prisons?

- Is someone who disobeys a civil law always wrong?

- How many people have been imprisoned unjustly?

- What are the relationships among prison sentences, poverty, and racism?

- Does being a prisoner mean you are a bad person?

- Do most people in prison deserve to be there?

- Are prisons supposed to simply punish people or try to help them improve?

- How come we sometimes imprison mentally ill people and other times hospitalize them? Who decides which?

- Are prison sentences different for rich people than for poor people?

- What is white-collar crime?

- Who are some of the famous people who have been put in jail in the United States?

- Why are protesters put in jail?

- What's an internment camp? Is it the same as a concentration camp?

- How often can people visit people in prison?

- Who determines what is punishable by imprisonment?

- How old do you have to be before you are eligible to go to prison?

- Is our prison system fair? Is it safe?

- Do juveniles go to jail more now than in the past?

- What usually happens to people who have spent time in prison after they leave?

- Why does the United States have such a growth in prisons in the last ten years?

- *If a country has more prisons than other countries, does it mean that country has worse people?*

- *What protections do people in prison have against violent attacks?*

- *Are the movies that show so much abuse in prisons very accurate?*

- *Is it harder to escape from jail today than it was in the past?*

- *Can people go to jail for getting in trouble in school?*

- *If you go to jail as a kid, is your whole life ruined from then on?*

- *What is civil disobedience?*

- *Do prisoners have any rights?*

- *Do many countries put rebels in jail? Do we?*

- *Is there a relationship between education and prison?*

- *Who should be responsible for crimes committed by children?*

- *What types of crimes are committed in prison?*

- *Should police be in schools?*

The list could go on and on. The main point is that teachers need to allow students time to build and share questions that might be good ones for the list. It shouldn't be a static list. As the unit progresses, new questions might arise that seem more important than the ones students came up with before getting involved in the material. The questioning stage is also the curiosity stage. It is the stage that builds engagement, interest, and motivation.

These questions will begin to develop into concepts and topics, such as justice, unfairness, disenfranchisement, zero tolerance, rehabilitation, courage, civil disobedience, cost of prisons, punishment or rehabilitation, and the nature of crime. One way to gather the evidence that might begin to accumulate on questions is using an idea from Sarah Brown Wessling, a blogger for Tch—the Teaching Channel (www .teachingchannel.org). Each student receives a manila folder with six library pockets attached inside and both index cards and sticky notes. As they read the material, students jot short comments on sticky notes and later return to those notes and copy evidence from the material on an index card followed by a conclusion or opinion statement. Next, they stick the index card in the appropriate pocket labeled with the concept or question, pattern, or character—whatever focus has been decided upon to sort information.

As the class investigates the material during the unit, the concrete form of these folders continually brings students back to the guiding questions that are the overriding issues of concern. And, what kind of material should students be reading and writing about? Collecting new as well as old material for student study helps to make broad overarching concepts more relevant and meaningful for students. Variety—types, degree of difficulty, perspectives—should be part of the collection of texts you decide to use.

Building a Text Set

A text set of a variety of materials on a given theme could contain visuals, articles, speeches, webpages, chapters or whole books, poetry, cartoons, music lyrics, selections of informational or fictional texts— the list is wide and limited only by research findings and imagination. I suggest you begin by gathering as much and as varied a set of materials as you possibly can. Visit **go.solution-tree.com/instruction** *to find a sample list of materials. This way you have ample material to actually choose from and needn't depend on one or two pieces you really don't think could be the best ones for the students, the specific skills and standards that are your focus, and for the time you have to spend on the unit. It's always easier to cut out pieces than to add them at the last minute.*

With a text set of materials to choose from and goals for what the study of the unit are to accomplish, I usually consider how I will order the material for students; how I will package it; what groupings I will use; what activities will best support both the material and the standards; what exactly I will want to have students do; and how I will judge the quality and evidence of their understanding.

Your focus will drive the concepts that students will be looking for as they read and discuss the materials, and the subsequent activities and assessments. Here are some of the possible uses for the materials in this packet that will be shared among four or five students.

- *Five pictures of imprisoned juveniles with biographies*
  - *Design a chart.*
  - *Fill in chart with information from the pictures and bios.*
  - *Draw conclusions, opinions, generalizations, and observations.*
  - *Develop a claim to prove or disprove.*

- *Mississippi school-to-prison pipeline articles*
  - *Jigsaw the reading among each student group.*
  - *Make a timeline of events.*
  - *Determine the cause and effect of zero-tolerance discipline.*
  - *Move the discussion from the student groups to the whole class using talking stems.*
- *Tables, charts, and photographs of growth in prison numbers*
  - *Write five questions (per group member) concerning the information.*
  - *Consolidate and choose the group's top-five questions.*
  - *Post questions for each group, compare the questions, and decide on the top five for the class.*
- *Bibliography of prisons*
  - *Divide the large list into sections so each group member has a set.*
  - *Look up the sites on the individual lists, and choose the top three.*
  - *Write which three sites are the best, and cite the reasons why.*
  - *Share findings with the group, and choose one finding from each of the top-three picks to look up, take notes on, and add to personal information finds*
- *Autobiographies*
  - *Read the education section in the autobiography of Malcolm X.*
  - *Read the first page of the novel* Monster *by Walter Dean Myers (1999).*
  - *As a whole group, discuss and compare the prison experiences.*

Once students examine the materials, they proceed to make claims. First they gather notes from all the activities and materials. Then, they select an area they feel strongly about and have ample evidence to incorporate. They use the thesis framework to identify their main focus, embedding evidence in the written paper on their selected topic or claim. Students should follow writing process procedures to revise and polish their papers. Group members rehearse presenting their claims and findings to each other orally and receive feedback on their presentations. Groups can then address follow-up challenges and questions, such as brainstorming what to do with new information and deciding on a whole-class as well as individual challenge to undertake. The following are some sample challenges and questions that might come up:

- *How can we share this material?*

- *How can we learn more?*

- *Who can we ask to come in and speak to us?*

- *What is the situation in our area? Our state?*

- *What are the statistics of juveniles imprisoned near us?*

- *What are the main causes of arrests and imprisonments of juveniles in our vicinity?*

The class can then brainstorm possible formats to use to address the challenges and questions:

- *Share information (poster, brochure, mock interviews, or school newspaper).*

- *Write lawmakers, advocates, and others for information.*

- *Ask various groups to come in and present information, give lectures, or suggest action.*

- *Debate juvenile incarceration in the United States and other countries.*

- *Skype a conversation with the author of one of the studies or books used.*

Students always conclude every unit with a reflection paper on the experiences, materials, discussions, and other parts of the study.

After dipping into the readings and collecting data or evidence from these materials that address specific themes or concepts, students are ready to begin making judgments and forming opinions that will eventually become the topics of their argument papers. A short piece from Ray Salazar's (2012) article titled, "If You Teach or Write 5-Paragraph Essays—Stop It!" contains three steps for leading beginners into writing thesis statements for their argument pieces.

1. *Make the topic specific.*
   - *Exactly who?*
   - *When?*
   - *How many?*
   - *Which ones?*
   - *Where?*

2. *Continue with a debatable phrase.*
   - *does . . .*
   - *does not . . .*
   - *should . . .*
   - *should not . . .*
   - *highlights . . .*
   - *ignores . . .*

3. *Explain the significance to the audience.*
   - *, providing that . . .*
   - *, resulting in . . .*
   - *, making us doubt . . .*
   - *, reminding us that . . .*

Facts are never an end in themselves. It is only after students have been given the opportunity to build up their ability to read, write, speak, and think of solutions to increasingly more complex kinds of problems that they will be able to take more ownership of their own learning. This is the essence of taking off the training wheels and creating independent learners. (M.K. Schreck, personal communication, April 27, 2013)

Conclusion

As you can see, the teachers featured in this chapter used a variety of tools to engage learners and provide rigorous, high-quality, standards-based instruction.

After reading through these lessons and units, what are your thoughts?

Choose one or two things you read in the lessons in this chapter that you might want to implement or investigate, and write them down.

The teachers featured in this chapter incorporated complex texts and text sets. They honored student talk along with less teacher talk. Their lessons were, for the most part, project based, and they included rigor that pushed learners from persuasion to argumentation and from memorization to understanding. The lessons demonstrate what you can do when you create powerful, rigorous lessons aligned with the CCSS and become a learner of your own teaching, allowing students to become teachers of their own learning. The teachers included culturally responsive strategies by connecting to student lives, including collaboration and group work, giving feedback to individual learners, and holding high expectations.

The next chapter examines formative assessment, feedback, and teacher reflection used as a feedback tool. In the midst of the delivery of high-value content lessons, we must continually ask, "What is the learner learning?" The next chapter provides multiple ways to answer that question.

CHAPTER 5

Use Feedback to Self-Assess Learning

> *Most teachers have not considered the "flip" in the definition of feedback. When teachers do, they begin to use techniques that result in gains for every learner.*
>
> —Jane Pollock

Jane Pollock (2012), author of *Feedback: The Hinge That Joins Teaching & Learning*, is an expert on feedback. In this chapter, she shares her current research and thinking about feedback and asks teachers to consider the "flip" in the definition of feedback and what that looks like in the classroom. Feedback no longer consists of generic written comments from teacher to student. Instead, learners need feedback that deepens their thinking and writing and moves them from persuasion to argumentation. To do this, they need self-assessment, feedback from peers, and feedback from the teacher. The CCSS require that learners be part of a 21st century classroom environment in which they use critical thinking in increasingly rigorous assignments, use technology as they engage in project-based lessons, rely on complex text and nonfiction text sets, collaborate in meaningful student talk rather than relying solely on teacher talk, and move from memory to understanding. One important component of being able to perform at these levels of rigor is the ability to use feedback to self-assess one's learning and understanding.

The flipping of the definition of feedback is grounded in the research of Hattie (2012), who writes:

> For feedback to be received and have a positive effect, we need transparent and challenging goals (learning intentions), an understanding of current status relative to these goals (knowledge of prior achievement), transparent and understood criteria of success, and commitment and skills by both teachers and students in investing and implementing strategies and understandings relative to these goals and success criteria. (Kindle location 3369)

Using Hattie's research, Pollock developed strategies for feedback that we describe in this chapter. Pollock's books *Feedback* (2012) and *Minding the Achievement Gap: One Classroom at a Time* (Pollock et al., 2012), in particular, inform this chapter. These two books are filled with techniques for improving learner achievement, and they support the work of English teacher Tiffany Holliday who, in this chapter, describes how she flips feedback in her classroom. Tiffany provides examples of student feedback charts along with her reflections about the improved engagement and achievement of the learners in her classroom.

In addition to Tiffany's classroom examples, this chapter includes a second kind of feedback—the kind of feedback arising from self-reflection. Self-reflection is an important part of the six-step framework because it undergirds each step of the cultural literacy journey. Without self-reflection, we cannot journey forward.

As you consider cultural journeys, think about the impact of culture on students' responses to feedback. Hattie (2012) writes that the culture of a student may influence the feedback effects. Students from collectivist cultures, such as Asian and South Pacific nations, may prefer indirect and implicit feedback or group-focused feedback, rather than direct feedback to the individual student. In contrast, students from individualistic cultures, such as in the United States, prefer more direct feedback in connection to effort, and these students more often seek feedback from teachers (Luque & Sommer, 2000, as cited in Hattie, 2012). In addition, students from individualistic cultures may become resentful if teachers do not notice and comment on their errors. They are more willing to try self-help strategies because they tend to be more goal focused on status and outcomes (Brutus & Greguras, 2008; Hyland & Hyland, 2006; Kung, 2008; as cited in Hattie, 2012). These varying responses to feedback underscore the necessity for teachers to be aware of the cultural influences in the classroom.

What might we learn from the feedback examples in this chapter? Usually we think of feedback as something one receives from someone else. However, in this chapter, we examine feedback in two forms of self-assessment: students use a template to self-assess their readiness to learn and, subsequently, what they learned. Teachers use a laser-like reflection on their interactions with learners. The chapter begins with Jane Pollock, who graciously accepted our invitation to write a piece for this book. In her piece, Jane reiterates the possibilities for feedback that students can offer themselves and their peers. Next, classroom teacher Tiffany Holliday shares the charts she uses, based on Jane's work, to engage her students and improve their achievement. In addition, teachers share how they interrogated the reality of their teaching situations. They reflected, sought feedback, and searched for where the responsibility for student engagement and learning lies—and their insights offer new ways of considering the role of feedback in our professional lives.

Flipping Feedback

Following is Jane's description of how she uses flipped feedback in the classroom.

When teachers ask me if there is one change they should make in the classroom, I respond, "Feedback." Usually teachers respond with a comment such as, "I just don't see how I can give any more feedback with my class sizes so large and so many students with special needs in them. Isn't there another solution?" The paradox about increasing feedback in the classroom is that the teacher does not have to give the feedback. Instead, the teacher just needs to provide opportunities for students to seek and receive feedback from others or themselves. The only way that can happen in the classroom is when the teacher is willing to slightly change his and her strategies to allow for students at every grade level to learn to seek and receive feedback.

In the book Feedback: The Hinge That Joins Teaching and Learning *(Pollock, 2012), I describe how teachers can modify behaviorist perspectives about feedback that purposefully direct the focus on teachers giving feedback to a more contemporary neurological perspective that includes an expanded definition of feedback based on research about the executive functions of the student's frontal lobe. To change the direction of feedback and expand the results, teachers could adapt techniques within their existing routines at the beginning, middle, and end of lessons by providing ways that students could seek feedback from:*

1. *Self—evaluating or using metacognitive strategies, seeking information or correctives, creating a self-teaching or self-regulating situation*

2. *Peers—clarifying information or processing aloud for confirmation, peer teaching*

3. *Teacher—informal interactions in class, questions designed to seek reteaching, corrections to assignments, test and project evaluations (p. 14)*

To make the changes in the classroom, I suggest that teachers teach students to use simple tools, such as the goal accounting template Tiffany Holliday shares in the "Using Feedback Charts in a Diverse High School Classroom" section that follows.

Most teachers know about the recommendation to start class by sharing the objective of the lesson with the students, but the goal accounting template allows students to learn to expect to interact with the goal at the beginning of every class. Whether in a first-grade or tenth-grade class, students can learn to write down a goal, determine a prelesson assessment score as a self-assessment, and then at the end of class score themselves again based on their judgment about how much they learned. This self-assessment not only provides focus for the students to engage but also allows the teacher to walk around the room to see how students evaluate their own learning. In many cases, it provides feedback from the student to the teacher.

Teachers who work with special education students, English learners, and students living in poverty successfully learn to use the self-assessment and feedback techniques as described in Minding the Achievement Gap: One Classroom at a Time *(Pollock et al., 2012).*

There are other techniques and tools to use based on the notion that students can learn to seek and receive feedback through pair-share, making their learning visible in note-taking that maximizes opportunities for feedback, and learning to generate questions, not just answer questions, in class. All of these tools are based on the results of meta-analyses that show the effect of feedback on learning as high—in fact, the single factor to improve learning. Most teachers, however, have not considered the flip in the definition of feedback. When teachers do, they begin to use techniques that result in gains for every learner. (J. Pollock, personal communication, March 15, 2013)

What insights did you gain from Jane Pollock's piece?

In what ways might you incorporate feedback into your instruction?

Using Feedback Charts in a Diverse High School Classroom

Tiffany Holliday teaches in a large, urban high school where the core classes often have forty or more students. Her students are fairly evenly divided into four cultural groups: Asian, Hispanic, African American, and white. Many of her Asian and Hispanic students are English learners and new immigrants. Challenged with diverse cultural groups, Tiffany was actively searching for ways to engage all the adolescents in her classroom when I first met her. My job was to provide professional development for the English department as teachers transitioned to the CCSS. What they wanted first was a way to more effectively engage their students. We used the six-step framework as a way to transition from their former instruction to a more rigorous CCSS instruction that included connecting to the students and building relationships (step 1); continuing to have collaborative professional development within their department (step 2); implementing specific culturally responsive strategies, such as the check-in, proximity, and group work (step 3); building more engaging, rigorous lessons that connected to the lives of the learners (step 4); investing in using the feedback charts with students (step 5); and continuing the professional development on Saturdays focused on cultural literacy (step 6, addressed in the next chapter, "Engage in a Cultural Literacy Journey," page 155).

During the first all-day workshop focused on transitioning to the CCSS, I was anxious to offer the staff anything that would increase their use of feedback for the challenging numbers of students they faced each day. I incorporated Jane Pollock's (2012) book *Feedback: The Hinge That Joins Teaching and Learning* into the workshop.

Tiffany, a third-year teacher, was excited about Pollock's use of feedback and wanted to try it in her classroom. In the following weeks, she implemented the feedback charts. Then, in the fall, she invested more time and effort into her use of feedback. She reflects on her use of feedback charts and how feedback changed her instruction and her students' learning.

I was one of those teachers who responded to the idea of giving more feedback to students with an anxious, perplexed look, quickly jumping to the conclusion that I was being encouraged to write more feedback on student work or find more time to offer daily, individualized, face-to-face comments to my classes of forty (or more) students. As I learned that Pollock's suggestion was not to give more feedback, but to find opportunities to increase communication (student to teacher, teacher to student, and student to student) and transparency of learning goals and progress, I was intrigued to learn more and try something new.

I began this school year using a version of Pollock's (2012) goal accounting template that another teacher created. I call it the self-evaluation sheet and refer to it as the SES in class. Students record the daily objective, rate their understanding of that before the lesson and again after the lesson, and finally rate their personal effort for the day. Toward the bottom of the document, students transfer their rating numbers to a chart to create a visual representation of their understanding and effort over a two-week period. After asking for some feedback from students about the usefulness of the form, I made some adjustments and created a different version (see figure 5.1). The new version has a different layout, a place to record what work is turned in on a given day and a back side for more specific reflection by students on their weekly learning, understanding, and effort.

Name: _____

Week of _____ **to** _____

Directions: Use the self-evaluation rubric to assess your work and behavior for this week. Then answer the reflective questions honestly and in complete sentences.

Category	Rating
Preparedness	1 2 3 4 5
Quality of Work	1 2 3 4 5
Time Management	1 2 3 4 5
Problem Solving	1 2 3 4 5
Attitude	1 2 3 4 5
Focus on Task	1 2 3 4 5
Effort	1 2 3 4 5

Total for the week: _____/35

1. The objective or standard I really learned and understood this week was . . .

_____

_____

_____ .

2. My greatest achievement as a student this week was . . .

_____

_____

_____ .

3. Next week, I will focus on the category of . . .

_____ .

4. I will know I am improving because I am . . .

_____

_____

_____ .

Figure 5.1: Sample self-evaluation sheet.   continued →

5. Last week I focused on _____ and I did or did not (circle one) improve because . . .

_____

_____

_____.

Name: _____   Period: _____

Date	Objective (Copied From Whiteboard)	Work Collected	My Understanding Before the Lesson	My Understanding After the Lesson	My Personal Effort for Today's Work
Monday _____			1 2 3 4 5	1 2 3 4 5	1 2 3 4 5
Tuesday _____			1 2 3 4 5	1 2 3 4 5	1 2 3 4 5
Wednesday _____			1 2 3 4 5	1 2 3 4 5	1 2 3 4 5
Thursday _____			1 2 3 4 5	1 2 3 4 5	1 2 3 4 5
Friday _____			1 2 3 4 5	1 2 3 4 5	1 2 3 4 5

Category	5 = Advanced (A)	4 = Acceptable (B)	3 = Adequate (C)	2 = Poor (D)	1 = Not Acceptable (F)
Preparedness	Brings needed materials to class and is ready to work when the bell rings.	Almost always brings needed materials to class and is ready when the bell rings.	Almost always brings needed materials but sometimes needs a reminder to settle down and get to work.	Occasionally has needed materials but might be missing some. Needs several reminders to get to work.	Does not have needed materials and cannot get work started on own.
Quality of work	Turns in work of the highest quality. Written work is neatly done and the content is correct.	Turns in high-quality work. Written work is neat but some contains errors.	Turns in work that occasionally needs to be checked or redone to ensure quality and correctness.	Work regularly needs to be checked and redone to ensure quality of work. Forgets to write name on assignments.	Work is not done or not turned in.
Time management	Routinely uses time well throughout class to ensure work is completed on time. Asks for extra time if needed before the due date.	Uses time well throughout class but may have procrastinated on one thing. Does not cause group to miss deadline.	Tends to procrastinate but does get things done on time. Procrastination may cause group to adjust work responsibilities.	Barely gets work done by deadline, causing team members to adjust work responsibilities or to miss the deadline.	Scrambles to get work done in the last few minutes of class after not doing any work for most of the period. Poor time management affects quality of work or group's ability to meet deadline.
Problem solving	Actively looks for solutions to problems. Works to make others' suggestions work even better. Checks class website when absent to determine missing work.	Tries out solutions suggested by others and occasionally suggests improvements.	Does not suggest solutions, but is willing to try others' suggestions.	Does not try to solve problems or help others solve problems. Allows others do the work for them.	Causes problems in the classroom or with group members that distract from teaching and learning.

continued →

Category	5 = Advanced (A)	4 = Acceptable (B)	3 = Adequate (C)	2 = Poor (D)	1 = Not Acceptable (F)
Attitude	Never is publicly critical of the project or the work of others. Always has a positive attitude about the tasks.	Rarely is publicly critical of the project or the work of others. Often has a positive attitude about the tasks.	Occasionally is publicly critical of the project or the work of other members of the group. Usually has a positive attitude about the tasks.	Often is publicly critical of the project or the work of other group members. Often has a negative attitude about the tasks.	Very negative attitude toward school and classwork. Places blame on others. Often extremely defensive when approached by teacher or peers.
Focus on task	Consistently stays focused on the task and what needs to be done. Very self-directed.	Focuses on task and what needs to be done most of the time. Other group members can count on student.	Usually focuses on the task and what needs to be done. Group members have to remind student to stay on task.	Rarely focuses on the task and what needs to be done. Allows others to do the group's work.	Spaces out or sleeps during class.
Effort	Work and classroom behavior reflect superior effort.	Work and behavior reflect strong effort.	Work and behavior reflect some effort.	Minimal effort demonstrated in work or during class.	No effort made to get help or complete assignments.

One of the most significant impacts that using this form has had on my teaching this year is establishing explicit, student-friendly learning objectives on a daily basis. With the use of this form, where students are recording the daily learning and language objective, I have become better at translating language from standards into statements that students can understand. At the beginning of the year, I told my students that, on a daily basis, they should be able to answer the questions, "What am I learning today?" and "How can I use that at college or work or in my life right now?" I keep these questions in mind as I write the daily objectives to ensure relevancy of the lesson. Having these objectives available for students builds their trust in me as a teacher because they can observe that I am organized and have a specific, measurable, and achievable goal for them each day.

Another, and probably more important, success based on using feedback charts has been knowing more about my students' level of understanding, effort, and engagement. I have developed a variety of ways to get feedback from the students to me from the forms. Sometimes I will do a quick survey of the class at the beginning of the period in which each student shares his or her "understanding before lesson" rating, and then I'll do it again at the end of class to see if the numbers representing understanding after the lesson have improved. I have had students calculate their average score for one of the areas and then write a reflection about what that number says about them. Students have also reviewed all the learning objectives for a week or two and identified one for which they could not answer the question, "How can I use that at college or work or in my life right now?" Next, they have written about what additional support or explanation they might need to determine an answer. It has been quite rewarding to witness the students having a much more clear connection to their own learning and effort.

As time progressed, students started not taking the rating part of the form as seriously as they did at the beginning of the year. This is partly my fault. I get so engaged with the day's lesson that I sometimes forget to leave a few minutes at the end of the period for students to complete their daily self-evaluation—and if it doesn't get done that day, the data are not as useful. I now have a couple of students from each class (they change each week) give me a three-minute warning so I can wrap up the lesson and allow students time to complete their evaluation.

Another challenge I have encountered has been centered around developing an efficient and useful way to review all the forms when I collect them every couple of weeks. I usually give students a weekly effort grade based on the ratings they give themselves on the back of the form, but I have not yet figured out a good way to evaluate their "understanding" ratings and, in turn, consistently change my scaffolding or differentiation in response. Overall, I recognize that the majority of students rate themselves higher for the "understanding after lesson" section, showing that they understand more at the end of class than they did at the beginning. This is good information, but I want to develop a better system for more closely analyzing their evaluations.

The possibilities are endless in terms of how to implement the use of feedback or evaluation forms. You can modify the forms to suit your personal style and needs—and those of your students as well. Something I might try in the future is coming up with an effort number that I think is appropriate for each student, based on my observations over the course of a week, and have students compare that to what they rated themselves and discuss or reflect on any discrepancies. This would help them understand what my perception of their understanding and effort is and how their body language or attitude might be influencing that. I have also considered having a teaching assistant input the numerical data covering a longer period of time in an Excel spreadsheet. This might help to solve my problem of finding a good way to consistently analyze the numbers. Students love competition, so finding a way to add that might help students keep up with rating themselves authentically and consistently. Perhaps a reward for the class that has the best improvement in understanding a topic or effort would work. I encourage other teachers to try some form of the feedback charts and find a way to implement them into your daily lessons. You will surely establish a better connection to your students' understanding, and your students will be better connected and accountable for their daily learning and effort. (T. Holliday, personal communication, March 2, 2013)

> *Tiffany writes, "One of the most significant impacts that using this*
> *form has had on my teaching this year is establishing explicit, student-*
> *friendly learning objectives on a daily basis." How has using the form*
> *caused Tiffany to be more diligent in establishing explicit, student-*
> *friendly learning objectives on a daily basis for the learners in her*
> *classroom?*

Tiffany understands the necessity of having students interact with the goals for instruction, and she has made feedback a permanent part of her instruction. She agrees with Pollock, who writes:

> When a teacher writes standards and objectives from the curriculum on the board, she should intend to have students interact with those goals, plan for those goals, and ensure that students receive frequent feedback during instruction and through testing so they can gauge their progress toward those goals. (Pollock et al., 2012, p. 40)

One of the many positive results of using Pollock's techniques of feedback is that feedback builds the positive mindset defined by Dweck (2006) in her book *Mindset: The New Psychology of Success*. Recall the descriptions of the first-grade teachers who taught their students how to self-assess and reflect using Dweck's work on fixed and growth mindsets. The power of the work of Pollock and Dweck together offers limitless possibilities.

> *What connections do you find between Pollock's work with feedback*
> *and Dweck's work on mindsets based on the descriptions in this book?*

The following Connect It strategy engages learners with the lesson. It offers the teacher feedback in that learners explicitly connect the standard to their lives, thus letting the teacher know they have made connections with the work and are more likely to stay engaged with the lesson and be able to connect new material to background knowledge they already possess. It also underscores visibility and voice because each learner shares with another his or her connections to the standard and the lesson, stating the connections in his or her own words and grounded in his or her own experiences.

Connect It

Use the Connect It strategy to focus students on the lesson you want to deliver. After you go over the standard to be taught, ask students to connect it to their lives. Give them thirty seconds with a partner to come up with how the standard connects to their lives. In what ways might they use the standard in their daily lives? How will it help them become more productive human beings? In what ways do they care about learning this standard? After they work through the connection with a partner, ask students to share their connections. Following are some ways to share.

- *Write the reason in an interactive notebook.*
- *Write the reason on a whiteboard to hold up in class.*
- *Write the reason on a sticky note, and post it on the board.*

Ask three students to share their connection with the class. Then begin the lesson. This activity can be done in two minutes, but the students' connections to the material hopefully will keep them engaged throughout the lesson.

Ask students to challenge you on how you selected materials to connect to their lives and cultures. Putting yourself out there is scary, but consider the respect for student voice you are demonstrating when you ask for feedback and suggestions from your students.

Using Feedback in Fierce Conversations With Oneself

As we ask learners to more honestly self-assess themselves, we must also ask ourselves to do the same. Scott (2002) offers tools for intensely personal feedback in the form of a fierce conversation with oneself. Scott writes that "we effect change by engaging in robust conversations with ourselves" (p. 246), and she offers the following questions to begin the conversation:

- What is real?
- What is honest?
- What is quality?
- What has value?

In the following feedback pieces, two teachers share intensely personal reflections in the form of fierce conversations with themselves. Jean Ducey is a veteran kindergarten teacher and mother of adolescent triplets. Elizabeth Hanson is a young high school teacher in Minneapolis. Both of these women decided they must have fierce conversations with themselves, and they interrogate the truths of their teaching situations with wisdom, humility, and a growth mindset. I am awed from what I have learned from their stories.

I (Jean Ducey) am a sixteen-year veteran of motherhood and an eleventh-year tenured teacher. I know my credentials don't in any way mirror a child psychologist, but I have begun dabbling a little in some personal reflection within my classroom around some of the tricky parts of teaching. You know what I'm talking about. Your mind has already gone to that child or situation that drains most of your energy. It's so tough.

This year, five-year-old Noah taught me more than I could ever possibly have taught him. He caused me to push my thinking past my comfort zone. Noah came in reading well past grade level for a kindergartener. His writing was conventional, and his analytical math thinking had already cracked the mystery of the base-ten system. He was a smart cookie—with quirks. He was a kid who marched to a different drummer. He had some significant identified needs. None of that intimidated me. I love these kinds of kids.

The first several weeks he blended in. He had blips in his behavior: outbursts during transitions, wandering the room, and not staying focused and organized. For the most part, he worked hard on his academics, and I made modifications within the room to help him be successful. All was working until we came back from winter break.

I expected re-entry from a three-week break would be hard for him. I was ready to redirect, stay relentlessly consistent, and shore up his behaviors—and I did. But I wasn't getting anywhere. The quality of Noah's work declined. His writing was haphazard and sloppy. His illustrations were drawn all over his words. I couldn't read what he had written. He began to vocalize more about what he wanted to do and didn't want to do. His preferred tasks were iPad, computer, and trains.

Anything else was a battle. I became frustrated and exhausted. I knew I couldn't let this cycle continue.

Maybe that was when the ah-ha *moment came. Noah was the same kid who came into my room in August—his behavior had just shifted. Why? How was I going to find out? I was nearing the edge of discomfort anyway, so why not take the advice of all the gurus out there and just lean into it? So I did.*

My classroom had a cluster of students with special needs. At times it felt like I had a revolving door of professionals who regularly streamed into my room. They were there to observe and note the learning and social behaviors of these learners as part of their individual education plans. I knew they had a wealth of centralized knowledge: speech, occupational therapy, adaptive technology, and behavior coaching. I decided to invite the behavior coach into my room to observe Noah and me. This was where the personal shift began. I had to open myself up to become a little vulnerable. I had begun to develop that gut feeling that perhaps, just maybe, Noah's behavior would change if I could identify my role in it. This wasn't one of those self-deprecating "It's all my fault" moments, where I was looking for someone to boost my ego. Rather, it was a move toward ownership. I actually felt safe in telling myself I had to accept that 50 percent of whatever was going on with Noah was something I had the power to change.

And so the observation came. Noah's day and behavior were typical as were my redirections, calm but with-it demeanor, and high expectations. I secretly wished that this had been one of his tougher days and thought at first the behavior coach was going to ask to come back. But she didn't. She praised my classroom environment, the safety, the calmness, and the strong routines. She loved the music, the visual cues, and the way we worked as a cohesive team. She noted the distinct improvements and growth she had seen from the last time she visited. And then she got down to business, and she hit the nail on the head: I needed to notice Noah more. He needed more positive interactions. I was so busy redirecting (in a positive way) that I had lost sight of a personal connection with him. I knew research says for every redirection you need to follow up with four positives. I had confused my upbeat, "Noah, when you do this . . . then you get . . ." with a positive interaction. No wonder the quality of his work was regressing. He was tuning me out and, in turn, tuning off from anything but his preferred activities.

I decided to become more aware of my interactions with Noah the very next day. I set my timer on my iPhone to go off every eight minutes. Whenever it went off, I would make certain to have a genuine, positive interaction with him. At first I felt like a fraud. It seemed a little contrived. Then I felt like a failure. Why wasn't I smart enough to think of this on my own? At one point, I felt overwhelmed: if Noah was benefitting from this, then who else would? Good Lord, was I a cheerleader or a kindergarten teacher? But what emerged was far gentler and real. I decided to create some simple stems that I could type and tape to the back of my name badge if I needed to for quick reference. "Noah, look at you . . ." "Wow, I noticed . . ." "You are working hard—keep doing . . ."

I kept away from the canned "I like" stuff, because, quite honestly, I knew some of what he was doing I wouldn't like. The goal was to be positive, not artificial. Slowly, after a few days, I noticed he was turning a little corner. We were able to string together a few good writing days in a row. Now mind you, they weren't perfect. In return, I noticed my own energy shifting. Noah took less of it so I had more to give. I naturally became more aware of keeping my positive interactions with others on my radar as well. I put my iPhone back in my purse. I didn't need to be reminded anymore. A self-fulfilling system was emerging. My 50 percent was a big chunk—like owning 50 percent of a company or 50 percent of stock.

And so, that ah-ha moment with Noah turned into a theory: how would the quality of my teaching and parenting be impacted if I went into my role being open to the possibility that I had the power to change 50 percent of what was happening across the board—the good, the not so good, and the indifferent. I've realized, once again, the beauty of how you can grow deeply as a learner while you are busy teaching. I am currently practicing this theory as I write. I call it Noah's Theory. Thank you, Noah! (J. Ducey, personal communication, March 3, 2013)

> *Reflect on Jean's story. In what ways did Jean use feedback as she worked with Noah?*

Jean uses feedback to learn about her teaching and guide her instruction. This needs to be the norm, not the exception. As Hattie (2012) writes, "That feedback is critical to raising achievement is becoming well understood, but that it is so absent in classrooms (at least in terms of being received by students) should remain an important conundrum" (Kindle location 3408). Hattie (2012) suggests we move from "talking less about how we teach to more about how we learn, less about reflective teaching and more about reflective learning" (Kindle location 3408).

To learn more about how students learn, Elizabeth Hanson attended a one-day workshop during a heavy snowfall in Minneapolis. Afterward, she approached me and shared some of the story that follows. I asked her if she would write her reflection for this book because I believe it is such a powerful example of how she learned to be culturally responsive to her learners. Elizabeth was willing to examine herself, as was Jean, and find what she needed to do to change her instruction in order to more effectively meet the needs of all learners in her classes.

This is a story about my personal teaching experiences and observations. I (Elizabeth Hanson) believe that all students are unique individuals and come with different ideas, values, and life experiences. In this piece, I make some generalizations about students in order to most effectively and efficiently portray my personal transformation as an educator.

I am a white woman. I am twenty-eight years old. I was raised in a suburban, upper-middle-class home. I did not graduate with any African American students. I did not have any friends, neighbors, or many schoolmates who did not look just like me.

I began my teaching career at Thomas Edison High School, a high-poverty, urban high school, in the fall of 2008. The student body consists of 96 percent of students who receive free or reduced lunch and is approximately 60 percent African American, 20 percent Latino, and 20 percent white or other. After consistently failing to make adequate yearly progress under Bush's No Child Left Behind Act of 2001, Edison High School had been "fresh started." All teachers were fired and given the opportunity to reapply for their jobs. Most teachers chose not to reapply or were not rehired by the principal. This is how I got my first teaching job.

The first day of school was a sweltering ninety-degree day. I arrived at school armed with 150 copies of a Sherwood Anderson's (1919) story "The Untold Lie," was way overdressed, and was completely petrified. I had never attended a school without air conditioning. My outfit choice was to be the first of many uncomfortable moments that day.

I was assigned to teach an eleventh-grade American literature course. Having been instructed not to do any community-building activities (in my education-preparation program) because "no one comes on the first day of school anyway," I asked for volunteers to read the short story aloud. I got blank stares. After an excessive amount of wait time, which quickly became awkward, I decided that I must persevere. I read the story aloud. Afterward, I had prepared a slide with discussion questions. I asked the students to respond to the first question. More blank stares. My entire day went on like this.

Seven hours later, the students left. I turned off the light and locked the door to my classroom. Sliding my back down against the door until I was seated on the floor, I thought to myself, "Well, this isn't going to work at all." I did not cry, but my brain never stopped buzzing from that moment on. This marked a pivotal moment in my career. They didn't tell me it was going to be like this.

I found a mentor, someone I trusted and respected, who was really, really good at her job. I read books on poverty, pedagogical theory, cultural studies, vocabulary, and classroom strategies. I participated in professional development courses on multicultural literature, encouraging active participation in classrooms, and ENVoY classroom management strategies. I went back to school to get my K–12 reading license. I drew heavily from the work of Lisa Delpit (1995, 1997) and Anthony Muhammad (2009). Geoffrey Canada was my hero. I rejected the implications in movies like Freedom Writers—*that if the nice white lady just works hard enough and sacrifices everything, her students will be successful—but I watched them anyway on days when I felt inadequate. I learned a lot about my own culture and which parts of my culture my students valued— and which they found boring or even oppressive.*

I went to basketball games, softball games, Hmong New Year celebrations, school plays, events in other neighborhoods, and barbeques. I called moms, dads, aunties, and sisters with good news and bad news. I wrote positive notes to my students. I spent hours planning lessons; watching my mentor teach; debriefing; asking questions; reading articles on teaching, planning, assessing; and always reflecting. The words of one of my university professors became my mantra: "Monitor and adjust."

My classroom became a well-oiled machine. We never wasted time. I greeted my students at the door every day and gave specific compliments in order to make them feel welcome and noticed. I worked tirelessly to make them feel valued and seen in my world and our classroom. I confronted them when they weren't meeting classroom expectations. I asked them to think, to be kind to each other, and to want more for themselves. I strove to give them the tools to be empowered in our white world. I gained a reputation as a teacher who never played—but who cared deeply about her students and got them to learn. I learned how to be mom, dad, teacher, friend, foe, therapist, ally, silent observer, or outspoken dissenter—and when to use which part of myself. I learned the value of relationships and that a look from me was the ultimate accolade or the harshest punishment. I learned the language of poverty. I learned what respectful relationships looked like between a white teacher and her nonwhite students.

I only learned how to teach students who didn't look like me.

Four years later, I accepted a position at a larger, more respected school in the district, South High School. This school has about 47 percent of its students receiving free or reduced lunch, 28 percent African American, and 47 percent white. Suddenly, I had students who identified themselves as black, white, Asian, Latino, wealthy, impoverished, and middle class. I was at a school that was truly diverse. I was hired to teach American literature to tenth graders. As a fifth-year teacher, I was now much more confident in my skills. I brought my Edison persona with me to South High School. I greeted all of my students at the door and gave specific compliments. When the bell rang, I expected students to be in their seats, working on their check-in activities. I tried to run my class like the well-oiled machine I knew it should be. Five minutes for this activity, twelve for the next. If kids were chatty or slightly off topic, I informed them that we would soon be moving on, because they were clearly bored. If a student had his or her head down or earphones in, I approached the student in the same way I had always approached Edison students: "What you are doing is a sign of disrespect. I am not disrespecting you. Put them away." I was intense and in their faces. In my eyes, I was the same amiable, engaging Ms. Hanson that I had always been. But these kids didn't love me the way I was used to being loved and respected. After my first week at South High School, I turned off the light and locked the door to my classroom. Sliding my back down against my door until I was seated on the floor of my classroom; I did not cry. I thought to myself; they didn't tell me it was going to be like this.

For the first time in my life, I had to learn how to teach a room full of students that exhibited true diversity. There were still kids who didn't look like me, but (all of the sudden) I was also being asked to teach students who did look and act like I did when I was a teenager. Even though the content was the same, the rules of this game were clearly quite different. These kids did not like me, and I did not like them. I needed to figure out why.

One morning in the second week of school, as I was attempting to start class, a student asked, "Hey, Hanson, why are you shouting at us?" I thought, I'm not shouting. This is just how I always start class. This sparked an epiphany for me: Ms. Hanson the Edison teacher was now in a new and different environment. Ms. Hanson the South teacher had not yet been created. These two personas were struggling within me and no one (neither the students nor myself) was winning the battle. I still needed to honor the systems and procedures (the art) of how I had learned to teach, but I needed to apply them differently here. I needed to find a way to marry my two distinct teaching personas.

I decided: I will still start class promptly, but I may give students thirty seconds to get their notebooks out before I start reminding them about classroom expectations. I generally try to speak in a much softer and gentler tone. Students neither like nor need to be yelled at to start their bell-ringer. They are going to do it. They just need a second to breathe before I get in their faces about reading, annotating, reflecting, and questioning. My new students are a little more standoffish. They have plenty of adults who love them; as a result, they don't run down the hallway simply to give me a hug in the morning. Other adults have already hugged them today. South students want very much for their teachers to share their personal lives with them. Edison students did not care about who I was or where I came from, as long as I had a plan. These are just a few of the differences to which I was beginning to monitor and adjust.

Students at South High School desire teacher approval just as much as my Edison students did—it just looks different in the classroom. They need rigorous instruction and teachers who care about them, teachers who see them. All teenagers (and adults) respond to specific compliments. They need someone to tell them when they're slipping and to help them tie the knot when they're at the end of their rope. They need the marrying of the Ms. Hanson of Edison High School and the Ms. Hanson of South High School. It's been a complicated, intensely reflective, and uncharted journey for me. Through it all, I am still and always will be working toward becoming a better practitioner. I am still acquiring the knowledge and skills to create a toolkit that will help me enable all kids to learn and feel empowered in my classroom.

What I've learned is this: I am a white woman. I am twenty-eight years old. I was raised in a suburban, upper-middle-class home. I did not graduate with any African American students. I did not have any friends, neighbors, or many schoolmates who did not look just like me, but I can and must teach students of color. I can and must teach white students. I can and must teach them at the same time, in the same classroom. This is when the real work begins. (E. Hanson, personal communication, April 16, 2013)

What did Elizabeth learn from her reflection?

What did you learn from Elizabeth's reflection?

Using Student Feedback for Teachers

Utley Middle School is located in an area outside of Dallas, Texas, and it is home to Hispanic students, African American students, and white students, with a small percentage of students from other cultures. Administrators in this school wanted to find out how students felt about their teachers, so they used a survey to assess learner attitudes toward teachers. After seeing the data, I asked three teachers—Stephen Ledbetter, Kristi Davis, and Christina Steffen—to share their thoughts on the feedback they received from students. Stephen Ledbetter is a math teacher at the school. I will start with his reflections.

I have been teaching for eighteen years, and I have always looked at myself as being the best teacher in the world. One day, I was looking at myself in the mirror, telling my wife how great I looked. My wife walked up to me and patted me on my tummy with a big smile on her face. I started to think; maybe I am not so perfect after all. When it comes to changing my teaching strategies, I had to make a drastic change. I opened up my file cabinets, which contained years of worksheets. I threw folder after folder away, until my two cabinets were completely empty.

I gave my students a survey that would help me determine my teaching strengths and weakness. After giving my students the survey, I learned that keeping students engaged helps them improve their content knowledge. One strategy I use to keep students engaged is technology in my classroom. I have students use Excel to design worksheets. For example, my algebra students use Excel to illustrate linear systems of equations. Once they have created the illustrations, students can determine the breaking point. Students learn to program cells to calculate mathematic problems. At other times, I get students to use prior knowledge to create a product that will help them understand the new content.

I received a majority of fives (the highest possible score) on the assessment. There were a couple of students that stated, "I didn't feel like he cared." Not knowing who the students were, I raised this concern with all of my students in all of my classes. I asked what they meant with this statement because I work with students every day before school, during homeroom, during my lunch time, and after school for those that need additional help. So we had a quick discussion about this in my classes to clarify these statements. I really work on my relationships with my students. I tell them that I treat them as if they were my own kids. I want them to be successful in life no matter what path they take.

I really address the ratings and comments on the assessment that I believe I need to focus on as of right now. I can't address them all right now—I'm just taking baby steps. Every year improvements will be an ongoing process. (S. Ledbetter, personal communication, April 1, 2013)

> *How is Stephen using the feedback he received on the student surveys?*
>
> *How might you add feedback to your practice to learn more about your students and about their perception of your classroom instruction?*

Another teacher at the middle school, Kristi Davis, a science teacher, shares her response to the feedback she received on the same student surveys.

When I was asked to give my students a survey about their thoughts and feelings regarding my class, I had mixed emotions. First of all, I was thinking, "I should have given the survey after a largely benevolent act so the students would be feeling generous." Nevertheless, I went ahead and handed it out within the confines of a normal school day.

As I sat down to review the voices of my students, I realized that the students were surprisingly candid, and many of them provided thoughtful insight. Of course, I did receive many surveys that were not usable, some were straight-line answers or were just blank. But the students who took the time to actually share their thoughts provided me with a perspective that I have internalized and will not forget.

One question, particularly, had quite an impact on me. Students were asked whether or not they felt as if I care about them as a person. Most students replied positively, either indicating, "agreed" or "strongly agreed." But one student took the time to reply to his answer of "disagree." He wrote, "She never talks to me at all." As you might imagine, this response stays with me. Has it changed my efforts in the classroom? You bet it has. I'm working to find ways to have meaningful interactions with every student.

Other feedback has certainly helped me to identify target areas, such as more hands-on activities, lab activities, and opportunities for creative expression, which I am actively incorporating into my course. Often, I refer to the survey while introducing a unit or activity. I might say, "In our survey, many of you mentioned your interest in being able to work with a group, so I would like for you to work together to . . ." I want my students to know that I really read their words and listened to their opinions.

Although negative feedback can be hard to hear, it is an invaluable resource for self-reflection and self-improvement. More than that, the answers you don't necessarily expect are the ones that really make reflective practice worthwhile. As an educator, and a human being, I truly want to be the best that I can be—so that I can lead by example and help others to reach their goals. If you aren't willing to take what is shared, reflect on it, and then make changes or modifications, you will not make progress in your classroom, your relationships, or your career. (K. Davis, personal communication, April 5, 2013)

In what ways did Kristi use the feedback from the student surveys?

In what ways might student surveys offer feedback for you as you examine your own instruction?

Christina Steffen, now a university administrator, shares a unique perspective on how she grew to understand the power of feedback.

Giving feedback and assessing my students? I admit I was lazy and not very good. As an art teacher you might think teaching was easy, and it was, for a while. Students make something, and you assign a grade—

it was all very subjective. I began teaching art in 1975. I closed my classroom door and isolated myself from the rest of the school. Besides, no one really knew what the art teacher did, or even cared! I planned lessons using the Madeline Hunter model. My approach was maybe a little too artsy. I would say to myself, "Oh, we could make this really neat _____" (insert drawing, painting, print, pottery, macramé hanging, and so on). I never asked, "So what?" I never asked, "What do I really want my students to know, be able to do? And above all, how will I know they truly understand?"

In 2001, my personal and professional life changed. After leaving the world of education for seven years, I went back to teaching. I was lucky enough to become part of a school district that was in the grips of complete change. One of the new superintendent's top priorities was to rewrite the curriculum districtwide using the model from Grant Wiggins and Jay McTighe (2005) in Understanding by Design. *The process is sometimes referred to as the* backwards approach. *I struggled to understand what it truly meant to craft big ideas to guide my teaching and a plan for ensuring the learning.*

At some point, and I'm still learning, it became apparent to me that the process of art—before, during, and after—could generate a sense of wonder and accomplishment that my students could transfer into other disciplines. Pollock (2012) writes, "The transfer of information is the hinge factor" (p. 4). I began to wonder how making art could transfer and how I could foster useful feedback and create formative assessments that were meaningful and promoted curiosity. The hinge became a journey to higher-level thinking and questioning that spans more than just the art project. As they process the process, my students began to think about their thinking.

Feedback is a funny thing. It can be as simple as writing a quick phrase describing what you've done, a thumbs up, or a lofty statement. Susan Brookhart (2008) states, "Some of the best feedback can result from conversations with students" (p. 15). This came naturally to me as an art teacher. As the students were making art, I traveled around the room, talking, asking them questions, and listening to their conversations. As I grew into wanting and giving constructive feedback, I began to ask more questions. Now, I didn't just say, "Wow that looks really good." I asked how they got there. What were the steps they used—and not just the doing steps. I was interested in the thinking steps. As Brookhart (2008) notes, "Feedback about processes shows students the connection between what they did and the results they got" (p. 21).

Feedback, great feedback, is a process in and of itself. What I have described should not be ignored if you aren't an art teacher. Rather, think of it as a path to thinking about the journey you take when you give feedback and assess your students' work. I think of feedback and assessment as a marriage. Both require planning, communication, honesty, and a little (or a lot of) risk. Every great relationship needs a little uncertainty so no one gets bored.

As I stated before, I am an art teacher. You probably are not. It doesn't matter. If we are to be global educators, our students need to be global learners. We need to ask students higher-level-thinking questions, and they need to learn how to ask the same kinds of questions.

Feedback begins before the lesson ever starts. My students know when they enter the classroom they are to assume the role of an artist, interior designer, art researcher, and so on. I might begin by asking my students what they know about the particular topic. If they have research or reading, I will ask them to use a 4–3–2–1 process: Describe four things you found very interesting. What three things did you already know or thought you might know? Develop two questions you still have about the information. Write one powerful statement using the prompt, "I wonder _____."

This process lays the foundation for them to start thinking about what they will be doing and begins a dialogue in their minds about what might happen. It helps me to know what they know—and especially what they are questioning.

Another before-feedback strategy I use is to ask simple questions after I have presented the introduction to a lesson. Because I teach art, I demonstrate a specific technique, such as how to construct a model, or show students a how-to video. The questions are a quick way to understand what the students are thinking. I ask them, "What are you most excited about? What do you think your biggest challenge will be? How will you decide what to do? How will you resolve your fears?" Crafting these kinds of questions is a framework for understanding how you can best help the student through the process. If you know what your students are thinking before a lesson, you will be better prepared to guide them to feel successful. As Susan Brookhart (2008) states, "Some successful learners are able to translate feedback about the task into feedback about the process" (p. 20).

As the lesson unfolds, whether it is hands on or not, I might give students an observation sheet, for use during part of the work. Here, I ask students to keep a record of sorts about their learning. The record can be constructed for all kinds of critical and creative thinking, depending on the lesson plan. I also make them take pictures of their work, from the very first day until the final product. You can adapt this to any lesson. Some have used their laptops and others use their phones. For example, figure 5.2 shows a decision-making matrix students used as they decided on a design for their weaving. They first sketched their ideas and, then, used the matrix to guide how they were using the elements and principles of design. They had to ask themselves, "How will I 'see' these in my weaving?"

	Line	Shape	Color	Texture	Space
Visual elements	Crisp edges	Triangle and diamond	Ivory, black, and red	Smooth	Created by line and shape
Pattern	Continuous to create motifs	Triangular and diamond	As above	Flat	Geometric
Materials	n/a	n/a	Kind of yarn	Kind of yarn	n/a
Balance	Geometric border	Triangle and diamond	Even spacing of colors	n/a	Use of spacing to create patterns

Source: Adapted from Swartz and Parks, 1994.

Figure 5.2: Decision-making matrix for weaving.

Each student keeps an ongoing data feedback record, which can be turned in daily. The decision-making matrix can be used at any grade level and in any discipline. You might construct the matrix to include options and consequences of the skillful decision-making process.

Students might choose an option and think through the positive and negative consequences of the option they chose.

Other questions I ask in the "during" phase refer to what the student accomplished the day or days before. Asking them to describe what they did and how they will apply what they learned helps the student problem solve. Making sure they recognize how to change something or redo portions of their work only strengthens the outcome. Example questions include: What have you learned that's helped you the most? What did you learn today that you can apply tomorrow? How have you changed your work today? These are the critical-thinking questions that students can learn to ask themselves as they transfer the skills.

Once students have completed their projects, I ask them to refer back to all the feedback data forms, observation sheets, pictures, and so on. I spend at least a class period asking them to write a final reflection and another class period discussing those reflections with the class. This process helps me reflect on any changes I might make the next time I assign the project. Following are questions I've asked for final feedback and assessment data.

- *What advice would you give someone that was just starting this project?*

- *Why would you suggest this?*

- *What was your biggest concern before you started?*

- *How did you resolve your fears?*

- *What were the biggest challenges you encountered as you worked through the lesson?*

- *How did you resolve them?*

- *What kind of thinking did you do as you progressed through the lesson?*

- *Why did you think this way?*

- *What did you feel most successful about?*

- *How did you push yourself to make this happen?*

- *If given the opportunity to do _____ over, what would you do differently?*

- *What would you not change?*

- *What if you left out _____ and used/did _____ instead? How would that have changed your final _____?*

Or you might give students prompts such as: "I wonder _____,"
"I think _____," and "What if _____?"

Because most schools and students have access to technology,
attaching photos of students' product before, during, and after makes
their work meaningful. Before demonstrating many lessons, I have used
the final feedback and assessments from previous classes to show the
students an array of student work. These are rich conversations that give
the students the opportunity to see where the lesson will take them and
create a sense of wonder.

Do you tweet? Do your students tweet? Twitter offers an excellent 21st
century feedback platform. I would encourage you to use Twitter in or out
of the classroom. There are many websites available to research how to
use technology like Twitter. Here is what I do: I ask students as they go
about their day to tweet what I call "random acts of _____." It all
depends on my unit and lesson plans. This is feedback for all 21st century
global learners. (C. Steffen, personal communication, April 17, 2013)

Christina truly teaches in a 21st century world where the learners in
her classrooms are expected to think critically and be creative, using
feedback to inform their progress and increase rigor. In addition, she
and her students use technology to support their learning. What ideas
did you get from reading her reflection?

Using Self-Assessment as Feedback for Professional Growth

The next piece, written by Teresa Bunner, connects feedback to the final step in the six-step framework—taking a cultural literacy journey, which we discuss in more detail in the next and final chapter of the book. A former English teacher in the Sacramento area, Teresa joined the Chapel Hill-Carrboro City School District to assist Graig Meyer with the Blue Ribbon mentoring program. The feedback element is less overt in Teresa's story, just as the cultural literacy journey is less overt than the teaching of an explicit skill in a standards-based classroom. This journey is truly an internal and often private one in which we use fierce or courageous conversations to interrogate our internal worlds. Teresa takes us on a journey from not knowing she didn't know to learning that the journey of cultural literacy is an ongoing journey to self-awareness. Feedback—using fierce conversations with ourselves and others—guided her in her work.

Twenty-two years ago, a young teacher entered her very first classroom. She had a passion to serve and a love of reading. She believed these were enough to prepare her to teach middle school in a very diverse school district in California. She said things like, "I don't see color. I treat all my students the same way." She didn't know what she didn't know, and she lacked any mentors around her who could help her with this. Yes, I was that young teacher.

Fast forward to today. I work as the academic support specialist with the Blue Ribbon Mentor-Advocate Program (BRMA) in the Chapel Hill-Carrboro City Schools. BRMA is a districtwide student support program designed to improve the achievement of African American and Latino students by promoting success in multiple developmental realms. That young teacher of long ago never dreamed that one day she would be working with a districtwide equity program. And in looking at my journey, it seems to be such a natural next step in my career.

Even as young and naïve as I was, I knew that somehow I needed more information. I was a good teacher. I had several award nominations and glowing evaluations to corroborate that. Yet, I knew that somehow I wasn't reaching many of those young African American, Latino, and Asian males sitting in my classroom each day. It would have been so easy to say it was them, not me. But in my heart of hearts, I knew each side held some of the responsibility.

When my district advertised a series of workshops on educational equity and diversity, I signed up right away. I was sure the workshop was where I would find the information I needed. I confess I attended two sessions and never went back. I left both sessions demoralized and feeling guilty because I was a white female. The presenters were not kind, and at one point when I questioned whether they were saying I couldn't teach my students of color because I was white, one of the presenters responded with, "You just need to understand that you are part of the problem." That response sealed my decision not to continue with these workshops.

But I never stopped wanting to learn and understand better how to serve students who don't look like me. Other than this program offered in the district, there wasn't much talk about diversity or equity. So I drew on the expertise of fellow colleagues of color. As moms and dads and fellow teachers, I asked them questions. I listened to them. I sought them out for advice. It took eleven more years before I gained the courage to pursue another professional development opportunity in my district around the topic of equity.

It was 2004, and we opened a new high school. A large percentage of the teaching staff was white, whereas just 13 percent of the student population was white. Our administrator, Terry Chapman, challenged us to think about the achievement gap and our own perceptions as teachers by having us read (voluntarily) a book called Courageous Conversations About Race: A Field Guide for Achieving Equity in Schools *by Glen Singleton and Curtis Litton (2006). Uncomfortable? A little. But here it was okay, because I wasn't being told I was part of the problem. I was learning things I didn't know I didn't know and dialoguing with colleagues. I was so excited and so challenged by this experience. I remember sitting in Terry's office one day pointing to the page that mentioned Chapel Hill-Carrboro City Schools. I said, "One day I'm going to work in a district like that!"*

And here I am—a long way removed from that young teacher who swore she didn't see color to an advocate for students and a passionate pursuer of equity. There is still much I don't know, but much I have learned along the way. I am blessed by the students, families, and colleagues who have helped me learn and continue to help me learn. Along the way I found my voice as an advocate for equity. I am thoroughly convinced we still do not openly discuss race in constructive ways that will bring about change in society, and I am more committed each day to fostering those conversations. I make friends and family members uncomfortable with my thoughts on race and equity, and I often must remind myself they are not as far along in the journey as I am. But each day, as I go to work where equity is my focus, I am more and more convinced that my long and winding path has placed me where I need to be—and I will continue to seek to know and understand what it is I don't know. (T. Bunner, personal communication, March 28, 2013)

In what ways does Teresa engage in fierce conversations with herself and others?

In what ways did this chapter expand your notion of feedback from teacher-to-student to student-to-teacher, student-to-student, and teacher-to-self? In what ways does self-reflection serve as a feedback tool for you? How will you incorporate different kinds of feedback into your practice as a result of your reading this chapter?

Conclusion

Are we using feedback to learn about how and what students are learning and what we must do to adjust our instruction? Hattie (2012) goes so far as to state:

> The major reason for administering tests in classrooms is for teachers to find out what they taught well or not, who they taught well or not, and where they should focus next. If a test does not lead to a teacher evaluating these claims, it was probably a waste of everybody's time and effort. (Kindle location 3461)

The role of feedback fits this definition. If we are not using feedback to learn about how and what students are learning and what we must do to adjust our instruction to fit the needs of the learners in our classroom, we are wasting precious time and effort. At the same time, this chapter expanded the traditional notion of feedback to include student assessments of teachers and, most important, teachers' assessments of themselves—or teachers giving themselves feedback through the power of their reflection, writing, discussing, and publishing of their most private thoughts about the act of teaching. The chapter flowed from public to personal, and it is a good transition chapter to move from the focus on the CCSS and standards-based instruction to courageous conversations about ourselves. Hopefully, the information in this chapter gave you some techniques, strategies, and methods for giving and getting feedback as well as providing models for self-reflection on your practice.

In the next chapter, "Engage in a Cultural Literacy Journey," we come full circle. We examine the journeys of diverse staffs in diverse settings. We interrogate the realities of their situations. We use the feedback to continue to grow in awareness of our journeys. We share how educators honor their voices through fierce and courageous conversations, showing love and honor for colleagues and for themselves, as they use the six-step framework to expand the implementation of the CCSS in order to give voice and visibility to every population that enters our classrooms.

CHAPTER 6

Engage in a Cultural Literacy Journey

Education is not for the weak-willed.

—Lisa Delpit

What are the pathways for a personal cultural literacy journey? In *Creating Culturally Considerate Schools: Educating Without Bias*, Kim Anderson and I (Anderson & Davis, 2012) examined this question and described a journey of several steps: self-examination, reflection, integration, actualization, and equity and social justice. These steps function as a guide for those willing to engage in a personal journey to better understand the influence of race and culture upon one's classroom instruction and interactions with learners and colleagues. In that book, we simplified the journey into four steps that educators from several districts used to learn about their own culture and its impact on the learners in their classrooms. The cultural literacy journey is *not* a program, and you do not have to adhere to it with fidelity; rather, it is a human endeavor filled with potholes, backward and forward steps, failures, and successes. The process is described by the educators in this chapter who walked similar journeys, using these steps.

1. They looked inside themselves and examined their own racial histories.

2. They listened to, learned from, and collaborated with others to learn what they didn't know they didn't know.

3. They read and discussed the writings of others (a list of the most helpful books identified by one district's staff is included later in this chapter) to integrate new knowledge.

4. They developed action plans to implement culturally responsive instruction.

Using the preceding four steps, we begin by looking inside ourselves.

Looking Inside: Our Inner Selves

We are often so busy in our lives that we forget to examine and reflect upon our inner selves. Take a few moments, and give yourself the gift of focusing only on you by asking yourself the following questions. Either write them in a journal or simply ruminate on them.

- What excites you?
- Who is most important to you?
- What are your favorite things, activities, or pastimes?
- Do you often make time for yourself and the things you like?
- How do you spend your free time?
- What percentage of chores at home do you do?
- Who controls you?
- Are you economically independent?
- Do you use assertive language?
- Are you angry?
- Do you use food, alcohol, or drugs as an outlet for anger?
- Do you talk about colleagues behind their backs?
- Are you secretly happy when your colleagues fail?
- Do you deserve more recognition that you receive?
- Do you attempt to manipulate others with your language?
- Do you create codependent relationships with students by saying things such as, "It hurts me when you don't do your work. Can you do that for me? I like it when you sit up straight."
- Do you expect administrators to read your mind? Are you afraid to express your true feelings to administrators?
- How do you express displeasure to your colleagues and to your principal?
- Do you feel in control most of the time?

- Do you understand the concept of equity?

- How does the concept of equity become personal within your classroom instruction?

- What must you do to make equity up close and personal?

- Are there learners with whom you do not connect?

- What is it about yourself that disconnects from these students?

- Do you hold higher expectations for white males and females than you hold for students of color?

- Do you agree there are many things you do not know you don't know about equity?

After you reflect on these questions, share your responses with a colleague, or write your general feelings.

Beginning the journey of cultural literacy requires us to learn about ourselves by interrogating our own biases. Many of these biases may be unconscious or implicit. In an interview published online with Rachel Godsil, director of research at the American Values Institute, she states that implicit bias occurs when "someone consciously rejects stereotypes and supports antidiscrimination efforts but also holds negative associations in his/her mind unconsciously" (as quoted in Roberts, 2011). This is possible because scientists conclude we have conscious access to only 5 percent of our brains, leaving most of our processing at the subconscious levels. Studies show that more than 85 percent of all Americans believe themselves to be unprejudiced, but researchers have concluded that most people hold degrees of implicit racial bias (as cited in Roberts, 2011). Godsil says that "because the vast majority of people consider racism to be immoral, they will be highly resistant to any message that suggests that they or people like them are racist or biased" (as quoted in Roberts, 2011). With that said, she suggests we appeal to people's best selves when working in areas of social justice, and we consider the cultural journey the work of social justice.

I thought I knew myself fairly well until I began to unpack my biases, examine them closely, and work to bring them to consciousness. Reflecting on my past actions helped me understand my lack of awareness of my own thinking. Graig Meyer, director of equity and volunteer services in the Chapel Hill-Carrboro City School District, helped me understand why that thinking was not crystal clear and conscious to me from the start.

I think a lot about intention and impact. As I started to become more conscious of the role racism still plays in society, I began to notice that when white people said things that hurt people of color, the white person's most common defense was something along the lines of, "I didn't mean it that way." Basically, they were asking for forgiveness because they didn't intend to hurt the person's feelings. But sometimes the white person would go farther, saying, "Don't feel that way. It wasn't meant that way."

I don't believe that you can tell another person how to feel. And I never once saw a person of color feel healing from a white person who responded that way. So I came to believe that we have to be accountable for our impact, even when it wasn't our intention to be offensive or hurtful. The point isn't what you intended to do, but that what you did hurt. Human decency calls for a sincere apology when you hurt someone.

We teach our middle schoolers about the difference between intention and impact. We tell them that talking about race is messy, and sometimes people are going to make mistakes. If someone says something that impacts you negatively, say, "Ouch" out loud (this is called the ouch rule*). The person who was speaking then has two choices.*

1. *If he or she realizes why what he or she said was harmful, he or she can apologize and then restate what he or she was saying in a nonhurtful way.*

2. *If he or she doesn't understand why the other person was hurt, he or she is responsible for finding out why. So he or she has to ask, "Can you explain why you said ouch?" and have a conversation. Once the person understands, he or she has to apologize and then restate his or her comment.*

It works pretty well, although students actually don't call, "Ouch," all that often. (G. Meyer, personal communication, April 12, 2013)

Graig's words help us to understand implicit bias and give us a strategy for talking about race, both with our colleagues and with the learners in our classrooms.

Uncovering Our Personal Biases

The cultural literacy journey is an exercise in reflection. Ask yourself the following questions to determine if you can uncover personal biases.

- Are there ethnic groups you shy away from or fear?
- If someone speaks with an accent, do you perceive that as an asset (he or she is multilingual) or as a deficit?
- If you have a choice to be with someone who looks like you, do you choose that person, or do you seek out those who differ from yourself?
- What do you do when confronted with any uncomfortable statement made by someone? Do you redirect the conversation or do you confront it?
- When someone is talking about the discrimination he or she suffers or feels, do you dismiss it or listen mindfully?
- Can you name your prejudices, even though you do not need to speak them aloud? Are you aware of what they are, so you can be vigilant in making sure you do not act out on them?
- Can you give others a break and not be quick to judge their actions? Perhaps the person who cut you off in traffic really did not see you, or perhaps the sales clerk did not know you were first in line. Can you give others a break, and realize that at some point in your life, you have done the same?
- Which kinds of students are your favorites? What kind of student makes you uncomfortable?
- Are you comfortable with present-day popular culture?

When I asked myself these questions, I realize that I usually do seek out folks who look like me because I feel more comfortable with them. I also tend to shorten conversations with those who have an accent because I have hearing loss and have to work harder to understand them; however, when I examine this bias, I realize this should not be an excuse. Because I want to fix others' hurt feelings, I have to work hard to listen rather than jump in and try to fix someone's hurt. Finally, because we were not allowed to discuss controversial topics in my home when I was a child, I tend to redirect the conversation when it becomes controversial and uncomfortable. None of these reflections is easy to admit; I have much work to do on myself, and this is what the journey is all about—looking inside and working on the inner self. As stated earlier, this is a recursive journey with potholes and missteps. We do not become perfect once we uncover our biases; we have much work to do to confront them and not act out on them.

Did your reflections offer you an opportunity to delve deeper within your culture and better understand it? The next steps continue to take you through a personal journey that includes acknowledging your ethnicity, nationality, race, and culture.

You can further investigate implicit bias using the following resources:

- The Implicit Association Test (https://implicit.harvard.edu/implicit)
- Implicit Bias & Philosophy International Research Project (www.biasproject.org)
- National Center for State Courts' "Strategies to Reduce the Influence of Implicit Bias" (www.ncsc.org/IBstrategies)
- Teaching Tolerance's "Test Yourself for Hidden Bias" (www.tolerance.org/activity/test-yourself-hidden-bias)
- THURJ's "Uncovering Implicit Biases" (http://thurj.org/ss/2011/02/1458)

Examining Culture

What is culture? *Culture* is the totality of ideas, beliefs, values, activities, and knowledge of a group or individuals who share historical, geographical, religious, racial, linguistic, ethnic, or social traditions, and who transmit, reinforce, and modify those traditions. Growing up in a particular context, you learned the cultural expectations for appropriate behaviors in that context or culture. For example, I was born into a cultural context that was white, Catholic, small town, segregated, conservative, and middle class. I learned the behaviors for operating successfully in that culture or context.

> *Describe your birth culture.*

Your *ethnicity* and *heritage* result from your ancestral heritage and geography, common histories, and physical appearance (Lindsey et al., 2003). My ethnic culture is white American with ancestors who came from Western Europe.

> *What is your ethnicity and heritage?*

Nationality means country of origin (Singleton & Linton, 2006). My nationality is American.

> *What is your nationality?*

Racial identity is how we identify ourselves racially. I identify as white. My son, who has a white mother (me) and an African American father, defines himself as black. In the United States, we are free to name our racial identity, no matter what our phenotypes—physical features such as hair, shape of nose and lips, skin color—suggest to others.

> *What is your racial identity?*
>
> *How similar is your ethnic culture, racial identity, and nationality to the majority of your students and to your colleagues?*
>
> *Think of your most challenging student or students. How similar is your ethnic culture, racial identity, and nationality to your most challenging students?*
>
> *Do you tell your students how you self-identify racially and culturally?*
>
> *Why, or why not?*

Sharing Our Racial Identity

Is it necessary to let our students know that we know and understand our racial identity? Yes, say authors Priya Parmar and Shirley Steinberg (2008). In "Locating Yourself for Your Students," they share how they relate their ethnic culture, racial identity, and nationality to the students and describe the positive results of such actions. They state that "when an educator's whiteness is unnamed, it remains in a dominant position, reinforcing that it is the noncolor color by which all other colors are measured" (p. 285). Good-intentioned white teachers often say they are *color blind*, meaning that they try to treat all students the same—or, in their minds—fairly. "Deciding that 'skin color shouldn't matter,' relieves whites of accepting the 'value imputed to being white'" (Hacker, 1995, as quoted in McIntyre, 1997, p. 126). When we hear someone voice that "skin color shouldn't matter," we often find that person possesses the privilege of white skin color. Alice McIntyre (1997) adds that "being color blind allows white people to both ignore the benefits of whiteness and dismiss the experiences of people of color" (p. 126). Yet children of color, usually very aware of their color and the difference between their color and their teacher's color, may find this stance alienating. This is especially true of older children who are further evolved in their own racial identity development. Parmar and Steinberg (2008) state that when "white teachers in racially mixed classrooms are unable or unwilling to name their own position in relation to the curriculum, they fail to engage their students in important inquiry" (p. 285). When white educators do acknowledge their positions of whiteness and what privilege that bestows, they will find that "students feel freer to discuss how they view not only the educator, but also themselves and the world" (p. 285). In other words, they are more likely to engage with the teacher.

If you are a white teacher, it is a good strategy to name your whiteness to your students as early as the opportunity presents itself. I do the same in workshops with adults. The result is positive with students and adults of color. When I acknowledge my white female perspective, I am acknowledging that I understand my position of privilege within a dominant white society.

In chapter 2, "Work and Plan Together Through Collaborative Conversations" (page 39), I touched on the white female hidden rules—the unspoken codes of conduct to which white females in the United States are socialized to obey.

> *In what ways does this information on white female hidden rules inform your cultural literacy journey?*

As a white female and a member of the majority group in K–12 public schools in the United States, I belong to the dominant racial identity group; however, my socialization differs from that of the males in this group (Bailey, 2001; Gay, 2000; Gilligan, 1982; Tannen, 1990). White women have been socialized differently in the United States. One way in which we have been socialized differently is that many of us were taught to defer to others (Tannen, 1990). We have learned well how to put others first, pushing our own needs deep inside our bodies. If you believe in the mind-body connection, you might believe that we push our needs deep into organs where illness arises as a substitute for the words we decline to speak, lest they anger those around us. To *defer* means to give in to the needs of others while harboring resentment and anger toward them. If this is a pattern in our private lives, we must examine our public lives—our classroom lives—to find if it plays out there in our classroom management, our community building or lack thereof, and our daily interaction with learners and colleagues.

If you are a white woman, how does your socialization impact the manner in which you relate to colleagues and to learners? Do you tend to defer and put yourself last? Do you bottle up resentment because of this? If you do defer to others and put yourself last, building up resentment, consider learning more about what you don't know you don't know about the place of white women in our society so you can begin to build the skills you need to assert yourself and create healthy classrooms for all learners. Ideally, our younger female teachers are being socialized to be more assertive, and we older white females are interrogating our realities. To build equity in our classrooms and in our schools, we must first be treated with equity.

Naming Racial Identity in Elementary Schools

How can you name your whiteness to elementary school children? If you have students create self-portraits, create your own self-portrait, and name your skin color. Or you can use this opportunity to point out that no one has truly white or black skin, but these are the names we use to describe them. You can use the opportunity to share positive comments about all skin colors and post pictures in your room of people with different shades of skin that range from the darkest to the lightest. Throughout the year, you can make positive comments about the people posted on the walls. In addition, your students will see their own self-portraits and have the opportunity to be surrounded by pictures that reflect their skin color as well as that of others. Of course, children's books are an important resource. With the aid of the Internet, you can search for children's books that deal with racial identity, and you will find several, such as *The Skin You Live In* (Tyler, 2005); *Shades of People* (Rotner, 2009); *The Colors of Us* (Katz, 2002); *A Rainbow of Friends* (Hallinan, 2006); *We're Different, We're the Same* (Kates, 1992); and *What I Like About Me* (Zobel-Nolan, 2009).

Consider reading chapter 3, "Why White Parents Don't Talk about Race," in the book *NurtureShock: New Thinking About Children* by Po Bronson and Ashley Merryman (2010). In the Chapel Hill-Carrboro City School District, some elementary school teachers are doing action research projects on racial identity for elementary school students. One teacher has written a master's thesis on the topic. Graig Meyer is an expert on racial identity. If you are interested in learning more about this topic and how to implement the work in the elementary or secondary classroom, visit the Blue Ribbon Mentor-Advocate Program (https://sites.google.com/a/chccs.k12.nc.us/brma/programs/seeking-the-self).

Naming Racial Identity in Middle and High Schools

In middle school and high school, you may have opportunities to discuss students' racial identities within the context of the class lesson, depending on what you teach. If not, perhaps you can raise the issue in a "final-five minute" format or during student group meetings. When a student brings up the topic, consider the following four steps:

1. Honor the student's voice and acknowledge what he or she said.

2. Ask the student how and when he or she would like to expand the conversation.

3. Acknowledge what you believe you are capable of doing and what you cannot do. For example, you might say, "I think this is a really important topic, and we need to discuss it. Remember, I am not an expert on race, and I admit there is a lot I don't know. For example, I can never know what it is to live the life of a person of color—or in your case, what it is like to be a sixteen-year-old African American male—but I can listen and learn." If you truly do not feel capable of facilitating a conversation about race, suggest to the students that you will bring in an expert who can facilitate the conversation. This way you acknowledge that the topic is important and must be addressed.

4. Use good communication skills when facilitating difficult conversations.

Supporting Racial Identity Development

Having thirty years of experience teaching in secondary schools, I search for strategies for working with race in the upper grades. One such strategy is to examine racial identity with students. When we share our racial identity with a class, we signal to them that we know who we are and are comfortable with that. Whether you are the mother of mixed-race children, as I am, or an educator who teaches students of any color, we need to understand racial identity development and the necessity for our students to understand it. Once again, I am fortunate to know and work with Graig Meyer, director of student equity and volunteer services, who is an expert on racial identity. In his district, teachers teach their students about racial identity and support them through the process of their racial identity development. Graig shares his knowledge of racial identity development.

Which comes first—strong academic outcomes for students of color or the students themselves having developed a positive racial identity? This is no chicken-and-egg question. We know the answer, and it matters a lot to the students themselves.

As a white person, I would have guessed that students develop strong identity traits as a result of successful educational experiences. In fact, I would be right—for other white kids! White students who succeed in school are likely to develop a positive sense of self in many ways. Unfortunately, because schools so rarely teach directly about race or active antiracism, white students' racial identity development is likely to reinforce the internalization of subconscious racial bias. Put simply, most white students come to hold the general belief that white kids are smarter than black kids. Further, they are also likely to believe that they are smart because of their individual effort, but that blacks struggle in school because of cultural (not individualistic) reasons. I hope that readers will agree with me that this is a problematic belief system. The good news is that it is not that hard to change. In fact, the same educational methods that will challenge the racial bias of whites will affirm positive racial identity traits for people of color.

Because schools tend to reinforce white cultural supremacy, students of color often find their racial identity battered even when they find success in school. This is commonly referred to in the much-discussed topic of "acting white." While some students of color find that they can maintain academic success by assimilating into the white cultural norms of our schools, it comes at a price of being disconnected from their own culture and sometimes even devaluing their own culture's strengths. Consider a Latina student who stops speaking Spanish, consequently losing the strength of bilingualism, becoming disconnected from her cultural group, and possibly never again being able to hold a conversation with her abuela.

Research on racial identity development has flourished since the 1990s, and it is fairly conclusive that for students of color, development of a positive racial identity is a necessary precursor for becoming academically successful. In other words, for students of color, the positive racial identity must come first.

In 2009, Mary Stone Hanley and George Noblit completed a thorough review of the literature under commission from the Heinz Endowment. In their report, Drs. Hanley and Noblit found:

> *The research shows that many children use their culture and racial identity every day in striving for success in school and life, only to have their race, language and culture disparaged in the process. Imagine the possibilities if cultural, social service and educational institutions worked with [families of color] and communities to help students develop racial identities and enabled them to use these identities to achieve in whatever*

context that they found themselves. Their culture would be a springboard to learn about the world, which would enable them to cross borders of knowledge and culture, secure in knowing that their understanding and experience is valued. (p. 7)

When students of color have developed a positive racial identity, it is part of the equation for helping them to find a path to success. In our work in the Chapel Hill-Carrboro City Schools, we have explored this dynamic with our middle and high school students. What I have learned from successful students is that they know they are living in a world where racism will create barriers for them. Nevertheless, they don't see their own race as a barrier in and of itself. They see it as a strength and an integral part of who they are. On the other hand, students who struggle in school are more likely to express negative attitudes about their own race and be more pessimistic about their prospects for successfully navigating and challenging any racism they will face.

Luckily, both the research and the students share some clear guidance on what they want adults to do to help promote positive racial identity traits. The research points out that culturally proficient pedagogy promotes positive racial identity development. The students corroborate this by calling on teachers to address race and racism openly and to build on the cultural strengths of students as part of their path to success. Student Maggie Respass explained it this way:

"I'm engaged when my teachers address race because they let me know that they understand that there's racism—but they're not going to let it stop them in the way that they teach. And so, when they become more comfortable with the racism issue, it helps me to become more engaged because I'm a minority.

"It doesn't matter if the teacher is black or white as long as they understand that there is racism and that they're comfortable with [talking about] it.

"You can't just ignore that there is racism in this school. So just saying that they love all their kids no matter the color . . . it's kind of like trying to ignore racism in a way. But it's cool that they love their kids, it's just that they're ignoring racism.

"My racial identity does matter to me because it makes me who I am. And looking at statistics . . . minority students are mainly the ones people

put down and make negative comments about. But my racial identity truly does . . . push me to learn because I don't want to be part of a statistic. And when my teacher addresses race, it helps me understand . . . you can keep doing this. You don't want to be a part of the statistics."

When I work with schools on promoting positive racial identity development, I always earn appreciation from a group of educators who often feel maligned or unappreciated, because I point out that the research also shows that using the arts is one of the best ways to promote positive racial identity traits. I love to see arts educators have their skills and talents integrated as part of schoolwide efforts to engage students. Once educators see this work, they love the way students respond.

I've seen an elementary school take on a "beauty project" where every student in the school created a self-portrait and wrote about his or her racial identity. I was amazed at the skill teachers demonstrated in helping kids in the early primary grades navigate this topic with limited vocabulary but unlimited artistic ambition!

At the middle school level, racial identity development is a very hot topic, because kids at that age are dealing with all kinds of identity issues, and race is often the most provocative. One of our middle school grade-level teams had every student read the graphic novel American Born Chinese *(Yang, 2006). Students and teachers discussed the book's exploration of stereotypes and racial identity development. Then students each created a graphic short story that reflected their own evolving racial identities and the stereotypes they struggle with.*

Students in our Blue Ribbon Mentor-Advocate program work with professional artists to create poetry, theater, and visual art that expresses their evolving identities. We introduce them to the critical race theory concept of counternarratives *and ask them to use their art as a way to explore the counternarrative they want to develop for their own success. We use films like* Freedom Writers *and a TED talk on "The Danger of a Single Story" as prompts for discussions about these important topics (Adichie, 2009). They show the art they produce to their families first, and then later share it with their teachers. The depth of their analysis and expression is humbling to those of us who sometimes forget all that young people are capable of.*

The feature box that follows shows a composite poem that a group of students wrote for our project, and I believe it gives educators clear guidance on how to help them along their path.

The good news is that teachers who explicitly address race and challenge racial bias help to develop positive racial identities for students of all races. (G. Meyer, personal communication, April 13, 2013)

I Am the Difference

I respect
but do not define myself
by the color of my skin,

Because the me that you see Is not the me that I am.

Let me introduce you to myself:

I am graceful, optimistic, and rad; athletic, courageous, and kind; creative, persistent, curious, and fun.

Every day I learn the truth of my story.

And whether you think I can make a difference
Or not
Is beside the point.

The point is not what you think
But what I do.

Because once, when I was at the movies,
In the mall,
At a restaurant,
In school,
Once, when I was anywhere at all,

A teacher
A mentor,
A counselor,
A coach,
Said to me: You have potential

Said: I'm proud of you

Said: You will succeed

Said: Never give up your dreams

Said: You can do it, you're unique, you're talented, you matter.
And all the other words we use to say: I love you.

I still remember.
It made a difference.
And I can pass it on.
I can make a difference
Because once I
Saw a student being bullied
Heard a kid who didn't speak the language
Saw someone on crutches
Met a homeless person
Saw undocumented students fighting for their rights

And instead of looking away
Or laughing
Ignoring it
Or acting like I didn't care
Pretending I was different

Instead of all the things I could have done
I calmed everyone down
Offered to translate
Carried her bags
Handed the homeless person my taco.
Stood up and said,
"I'm undocumented, too."

You can keep power for yourself
Or you can pass it on
I know which makes you stronger.

Keep moving forward.
I have a purpose here.
I can make a difference
Because it's something I've already done.

How about you?

The poem written by a group of students declares their individuality and their solidarity. Graig and his work on racial identity development support the district's students of color as well as all students in learning about their own racial identities. They are strong, and they are ready to make a difference in their own lives and in the lives of others.

The stories told next illustrate ways in which adults have embarked upon this journey.

Journeying With Whole-School Involvement

This section features three descriptions of whole-staff cultural literacy journeys. The first is a big-picture description of an entire district's journey to cultural literacy. The district staff began its journey many years ago and continues today. The second description is of a single staff in an elementary school—an "up close and personal" piece. The final description is the work being done at a large rural high school initiated by an assistant principal and the director of student services in the district. These descriptions offer you and your professional learning groups the opportunity to take the four steps of looking inside, learning with others, learning from others, and creating an action plan for implementation. Let's begin with the journey taken by the Chapel Hill-Carrboro School District.

Journeying to Equity and Excellence in the Chapel Hill-Carrboro City Schools

The Chapel Hill-Carrboro City Schools have had a strategic focus on improving the achievement of students of color since 1993. In that year, the district first disaggregated achievement scores by race and commissioned a Blue Ribbon Task Force on the achievement of African American students. The task force made nearly one hundred recommendations that the school district pursued in subsequent years. In 2000, the district updated its efforts with a new study commission and strategic plan for improving the achievement of both African American and Latino students. In 2008, the district created a new strategic plan that includes a "Commitment to Excellence and Equity" alongside the district's mission and vision. Beginning in 2012, the district has made additional steps to integrate its core equity values and practices into the instructional model and curriculum.

The district's focus has been led by the superintendent and school board, who have placed closing the achievement gap at the top of the strategic goals every year.

Under their leadership, the district has implemented a sustained effort for equity and excellence in their schools.

This initiative calls for increasing the achievement of all students, narrowing the gap in performance by accelerating the improvement of low-performing groups, and eliminating the racial predictability of academic performance. Striving for equity requires the district to provide adequate resources to all students based on their individual learning needs and keeps the focus on high expectations for excellence for students no matter their background.

A sustained staff development program has built awareness and developed skills for every staff person in the district. Individual schools are required to include specific plans for improving the achievement of students of color as part of their school improvement planning. District resources have been dedicated to programs such as Advancement Via Individual Determination (AVID), Blue Ribbon Mentor-Advocate, Parent University, and English learner staffing in order to provide targeted support to students of color. The district has relied on two forms of outside support to deepen its work. It is a founding member of the Minority Student Achievement Network (MSAN), a coalition of twenty-five suburban and college-town school districts that are generally high achieving but struggle with a significant minority achievement gap. The district benefits from this partnership through the opportunities it provides for learning from the experiences of similar districts in different areas of the country. The district has also had an ongoing partnership with the Pacific Educational Group. The work with Glenn Singleton and his colleagues has helped the district develop capacity for courageous conversations about the intersection of race and education and an awareness of the role that institutionalized racism plays in perpetuating the struggles of students of color and the general success of white students.

School district educators, community allies, and other outside service providers are encouraged to add to the evolving work in this area. The district welcomes multiple perspectives on how to best serve students of color. It asks that partners honor and support efforts to engage every educator in moving beyond a color blind paradigm, creating a culturally proficient educational environment where the race and culture of every student is seen as bringing value to the educational experience. The expectation is that educators will take responsibility for their role in educating all students rather than relying on insufficient explanations for failure based on the student's race, economic status, language skills, or family situation. The district believes that students of color are capable of the same academic excellence as anyone else, and it continues to work on creating a learning environment where all students fulfill their potential. Visit **go.solution-tree.com/instruction** for additional information about the district's journey.

The staff in the Chapel Hill-Carrboro City School District read and discussed the core texts in the following feature box during their cultural journeys (annotated by Graig Meyer, director for student equity and volunteer services).

Core Texts for Racial Equity

Davis, Bonnie. (2006; 2nd edition, 2012). How to Teach Students Who Don't Look Like You: Culturally Responsive Teaching Strategies. *This book is a guide to reflective practice for working effectively with students of different races and cultures from your own.*

Delpit, Lisa. (1995). Other People's Children: Cultural Conflict in the Classroom. *Delpit provides a seminal and critical look at how race and culture impact schooling. The book is especially helpful for examining why educators so rarely talk openly about race.*

Hanley, Mary Stone, and Noblit, George. (2009). Cultural Responsiveness, Racial Identity, and Academic Success: A Review of Literature. *This thorough overview of the research connecting race and student achievement was commissioned by the Heinz Foundation.*

Howard, Gary R. (1999). We Can't Teach What We Don't Know: White Teachers, Multiracial Schools. *Howard provides a very personal look at the complexities of being a white educator trying to address racial issues.*

Ladson-Billings, Gloria. (1994). The Dreamkeepers: Successful Teachers of African American Children. *Ladson-Billings describes how some teachers (of all races) have been successful with African American students.*

Perry, Theresa, Hilliard, Asa, and Steele, Claude. (2003). Young, Gifted, and Black: Promoting High Achievement Among African-American Students. *Perry advances a theory about how and why African Americans excel in education. Steele discusses the impact of "stereotype threat." Hilliard examines how we can close the achievement gap by using tools, skills, and knowledge that we already have in our possession.*

Singham, Mano. (1998). "The Canary in the Mine: The Achievement Gap Between Black and White Students." Phi Delta Kappan, *Vol. 80, No. 1. Singham debunks many of the myths commonly used to explain why students of color are not learning. He provides examples of how schools can be responsible for overcoming external barriers to success.*

Singleton, Glenn, and Linton, Curtis. (2006). Courageous Conversations About Race: A Field Guide for Achieving Equity in Schools. *The authors provide a field guide for educators who want to explore race and equity in a professional context. Includes staff development activities.*

Tatum, Beverly Daniel. (1997). "Why are All the Black Kids Sitting Together in the Cafeteria?" and Other Conversations About Race. *This book is an excellent primer for understanding racial identity development of all students.*

The work in Chapel Hill-Carrboro continues today because educators truly believe that there is no closure to this work. They continue to examine themselves, listen and learn with others, learn from others, and embed culturally responsive strategies into their instruction. Visit **go.solution-tree.com/instruction** to find links to additional materials from Chapel Hill-Carrboro.

The next journey is that of a single elementary school with a staff who courageously undertook a cultural literacy journey.

Journeying Up Close and Personal With North Glendale Elementary School

North Glendale Elementary School prides itself on the high academic achievement of its students and the professionalism of its staff. All of the 2012–2013 classroom teachers were white females, and the principal was a white male (prior to 2012–2013, there had been one white male classroom teacher). Four years prior, this staff chose to embark on a personal journey to better understand the achievement gaps they found when they disaggregated the data from state test scores. Why were their Latino and African American learners underperforming their white learners? Under the direction of principal Todd Benben, literacy coach and reading specialist Roberta McWoods, and fifth-grade classroom teacher Damian Pritchard, a few staff members chose to begin their work in a small, volunteer group reading and discussing *Courageous Conversations About Race* (Singleton & Linton, 2006). At the end of the first year, the group decided to continue the book study but with the entire staff. The staff continued to meet after school one Monday a month, and they did this until they finished the book in the fall of their fourth year on the journey. The reasons it took so long to read this book are many and varied. The group met approximately six times a year, and they found the material challenging, so they chose to spend several meetings on specific chapters. They included courageous conversations about current topics along the way and moved from whole-group discussion to small-group discussion, repeating some material in the new format. This speaks to their endurance!

The steps they took included reading the following books during the years noted:

- Volunteer book study on *Courageous Conversations About Race* (2008–2009)
- Mandatory all-staff book study on *Courageous Conversations About Race* (2009–2010; 2010–2011; 2011–2012)
- Volunteer book study on *Conscious Discipline* (Bailey, 2001; 2011–2012; 2012–2013)
- Continued conversations about race, culture, class, using *How to Teach Students Who Don't Look Like You: Culturally Responsive Teaching Strategies* (Davis, 2012; 2012–2013)

The educators at North Glendale understand, as do the educators in the Chapel Hill-Carrboro City School District, that the journey *never* ends; therefore, they continue to reflect on their journeys throughout the process. A set of questions were given to staff about halfway through the book study, and another set was distributed at the end of the book study in the fall of 2012. In addition, following are questions asked of the leaders of the journey after the staff completed the book study of *Courageous Conversations About Race*. The responses to these questions are provided in written form and interviews later in this chapter. These educators' responses offer insight into the personal growth experienced by the staff.

Describe the personal cultural journey you took over the past four years with the staff at North Glendale:

1. What were the outcomes for the equity work using Glenn Singleton's and Curtis Linton's book, *Courageous Conversations About Race*?

2. What are some of the challenges integrating equity work (and this book study) into a focus on instruction for the staff? What are some possible ways it can work?

3. Knowing what you know now, what things would you have done differently?

4. What things worked especially well?

5. What things did not work?

6. In what ways did the journey most change you?

7. In what ways have you remained unchanged by this work/journey?

8. In what ways did the cultural work build community among the staff? Give concrete examples.

9. In what ways did the cultural work cause rifts among staff members?

10. Describe the equity lens you feel is currently in place at North Glendale.

11. What do you still want to name and get better at in the area of equity for all students? What do you still want to change?

12. What named goals are linked to student achievement?

Midway through the book study, project leaders sent a questionnaire to staff. The professional development learning goals were to:

- Have conversations that can point us in the right direction by engaging, sustaining, and deepening the conversation about race, racial identity development, and institutional racism.

- Create a lasting foundation on which magnificent new relationships between teacher and student are built and higher achievement is gained.

The following are some of their responses to the questionnaire.

1. What is your overall assessment of whether the learning goals were met?

1 (2 people)	2 (3 people)	3 (13 people)	4 (8 people)
The learning *began* to address the learning goals.	The learning *approached* meeting the goals.	The learning goals *were met*.	The learning goals were *surpassed*.

Respondents made comments such as: "I liked working in small groups. I feel I was more comfortable and could speak my truth." "Loved the small groups! The smaller group enabled me to share more freely." "We're not there yet. I still feel some discomfort in my group." "I think it was good. We will never get to where we, as individuals and staff, want to be. This is a good start."

2. Did you learn something new? Did you gain new skills and/or understandings?

1 (0 people)	2 (2 people)	3 (15 people)	4 (9 people)
I cannot think of anything that was actually new to me (skill or understanding).	I learned just a little something new.	Yes, I learned something new. I learned new skills and/or understandings.	Yes, I learned something new. I gained new skills and/or understandings that surpassed what I expected.

Respondents made comments such as: "Great way to think about strategies—Bonnie's structure of macro culture, as well as traits of the oppressed." "In trying to speak my truth, I still feel judged at times—verbally in the group. It is not safe yet." "I gained a new perspective on one of my African American students and how I can make a more positive connection with him and his family." "I more clearly understand my participation as a nondominant culture community member."

3. Was what you learned valuable to your classroom and valuable to your teaching effectiveness?

1 (0 people)	2 (4 people)	3 (13 people)	4 (9 people)
I cannot think of anything that was really valuable to me or valuable to my teaching effectiveness.	The learning approached being valuable for my classroom and my teaching effectiveness. Perhaps it is too soon to tell.	Yes, what I learned is valuable for my classroom and my teaching effectiveness.	Yes, what I learned is valuable for my classroom and my teaching effectiveness. The overall learning surpassed what I expected.

Respondents made comments such as: "I can always apply something new to my teaching to be more aware of how I talk to/teach my students of color and white students." "I'm more aware with my children of color, but I'm not sure what else to do." "These are things that I can use every day or can make me more aware of race and how I can change for the better to improve student learning."

4. Will your new learning contribute to an increase in student achievement?

1 (0 people)	2 (7 people)	3 (11 people)	4 (7 people)
I cannot think of any ways in which this learning will increase student achievement.	I am not sure if there will be evidence that student achievement will increase. I will be watching.	I think there will be evidence that student achievement will increase.	I think there will be evidence that student achievement will increase. I think the evidence will be impressive.

Respondents made comments such as: "I hope—every day—I think this is the point." "I work hard with all children." "This is why we are meeting!"

5. Building our capacity and discovering our collective strengths are important in our ongoing professional learning. Did you learn from colleagues during this professional growth opportunity?

1 (0 people)	2 (2 people)	3 (12 people)	4 (11 people)
I cannot think of anything that I actually learned from colleagues.	Yes, I learned a few things from colleagues.	Yes, the experience provided the opportunity to learn from colleagues.	Yes, the experience provided the opportunity to learn from colleagues, and the learning surpassed what I might have expected.

Respondents made comments such as: "Yes, I feel that we have many strengths." "Very good discussion." "Working in small groups was really helpful—accomplished more than I expected."

6. What is the first thing you will do as a result of this new learning?

- Increase contact time with African American parents (with phone calls and so on).
- Keep an open mind and continue to be an observer of others.
- Continue to attempt open conversations about race and questions that I as a classroom teacher have.

- Continue to evaluate my interactions with adults and students of color.
- Start thinking about building relationships—with all students and parents.

7. What questions do you have as a result of this new learning?
- I question myself continuously. I always thought it was self-doubt, but I am realizing maybe it is growth.
- What are some specific ways to make our African American families feel welcomed?
- How do I continue to learn what I don't know?
- What do I do inadvertently that builds walls instead of bridges?
- How can I learn more about cultures—gender and race differences?

8. What additional information or support do you need to enhance the meaning and use of this new learning?
- Continue to study as a group
- More voices from African Americans
- More small-group talking with different people
- To have my voice heard

9. What improvements do you recommend for this professional development time?
- More time
- More in-building time to work with teammates
- Nothing—this was great!
- Did not like the big-group dynamic, but it's interesting to hear responses. I don't feel safe with my feelings.

This assessment, done a little more than halfway through the personal cultural journey, emphasized the participants' desire for small groups rather than the large group format used at the onset of the book study. Once small groups were instituted, participants began to share more openly; at the same time, they had learned more, but there appears to be a real desire to keep the sharing in small groups due to the dynamics of the female teachers on the staff. To better understand these dynamics, we focused on white women, using the books *Conscious Discipline* (Bailey, 2001) and *How to Teach Students Who Don't Look Like You* (Davis, 2012); both of these books include information on how white women engage learners and their colleagues.

At the end of the journey (knowing always that there is no *real* end), staff received another assessment, written anonymous reflections. A sampling of these reflections follows.

The last four years have been invaluable. I didn't know what I didn't know about teaching students of color before this began. I now know that there is so much to know and that we must continue this learning. The statement, "How often do we make students feel less than?" is a powerful reminder that we must be educated about how we talk to our students of all races. As Peter Johnston (2012) reminds us in Open Minds: Using Language to Change Lives, *we should use choice words— words that don't bite or demean or sting the soul of a student. Wow! I can't wait to get into the next phase of our journey.*

I have loved spending the past four years having courageous conversations with our staff. I have seen such growth in myself and many of the staff members since we started down this path. I wouldn't want to work anyplace else!

As our staff summarized and discussed the final chapters of the book Courageous Conversations *(Singleton & Linton, 2006), we openly and honestly evaluated our journey of meeting the needs of all children, and, in particular, our children of color. One of the most interesting questions raised during our discussion was, "Do any of our students feel 'less than'?" The staff continues to be motivated to learn, grow, and provide the best possible instruction with an open mindset.*

I thought our afternoon discussing the end of the Courageous Conversations *book was definitely time well spent. I am excited to continue learning more about the staff and our high expectations and commitments to all children. As a first-year teacher, I can say that I'm thrilled to be part of a staff that is willing and determined to have these courageous conversations. I hope to continue to learn more about myself and changes I can make to work toward closing the achievement gap.*

I showed up at the babysitter's Friday afternoon, and she asked, "So, how was the staff development?" It was easy to answer this question. I replied, "We finished our multiyear book study, but we are going to continue to meet as a staff to focus on meeting the needs of all students, especially those that don't look like me." Friday was valuable for me as a parent, a wife, a friend, a colleague, and a teacher. It was time well spent growing and learning with my peers. If only all staff development was like this!

I realize, for myself, I've come a long way in this journey. There are so many times I would like "do-overs" from the past. I still continue to be disappointed in myself for handling some things the way I do, but children of color are in the forefront of my mind every day. It's a journey that will continue the rest of my life. And that's a good thing!

Even though I came into this book study toward the end, these few professional development days have been extremely meaningful (becoming aware of the existing diversity in our classrooms and community). To be honest . . . until this book study, I was unaware (maybe blinded is a better word) by the white privilege I have grown up with. That's not OK. Thanks to these discussions and activities, I will consciously (and hopefully subconsciously) become more aware of making everyone feel welcome, respected, and equal in my classroom— both students and families.

The fact that we have kept our focus on this topic for three years is really paying dividends. The richness and depth of the work are evident. New staff realize that this is part of our culture. This is a model for the district—pick a focus and keep it as a focus for multiple years—adding to it along the way.

Turning Points in the Journey

At times along this journey, the staff became bogged down; then, something would occur that would cause a shift in the thinking and doing of the staff. Following are catalysts for these shifts.

- When the groups moved from one large discussion group into small groups, participants opened up and shared in new ways.
- When the group discussed scenarios relevant to the school—things that actually happened at the school, such as action research by the fifth-grade African American boys and the soul food luncheon—staff once again began to share more openly and honestly.
- When the guidance counselor shared his personal epiphany about the impact of race on his adopted sons, the staff expanded their understanding of the impact of race on their interactions with others (Davis, 2012).

Keith Price, the assistant principal for 2012–2013 and former physical education teacher at the school for many years, is one of the most vocal staff members concerning his cultural journey. Several times he has shared with others how much he has learned and changed as a result of the equity work at North Glendale. In Keith's case, it was a matter of what he didn't know he didn't know, and as he grew in awareness, he opened up and often shared his feelings with the large group. In a later interview, Keith shared the following insights.

> Because of the knowledge I have received on this journey, I now see students and staff as individuals. I establish relationships with each so that I can understand them and they can understand me. What works? Walking in all classrooms every day—being visible. Three years ago I would have never noticed that black kids are treated differently. Now I see it almost on a daily basis. (K. Price, personal communication, March 13, 2013)

An Outside Perspective

As one of the facilitators of the book study, Damian Pritchard holds a unique perspective. he is British and not a U.S. citizen, and he is a white male—one of two male classroom teachers during the first three years and the sole male during the fourth year. He now is the teacher for the gifted students in the building. Damian shares his thoughts and feelings about the journey of the staff over more than three years in an interview.

What worked during this cultural journey with the staff? We committed to it (the book study using Courageous Conversations About Race, *Singleton & Linton, 2006) and didn't abandon ship. Requiring us to stick with it is the important piece. Having the voices of African Americans on staff and an outside facilitator allowed it to work. We had principal support, no undermining or making excuses from our principal, who really does live his beliefs. He didn't let us say we're going to have a conversation once a month and forget about it. It became part of our culture. It wasn't just isolated. The conversations continued outside of meeting, added to weekly work, and so on.*

We also had a willingness of staff to commit to conversations about race—to actually be honest about how they were; we have some staff members who were resistant and sometimes prevented the conversation going forward, but as the staff changed, the comments became fewer.

We also listened. My knowledge is still very incomplete. The way I learn is by absolute listening and reflecting—and thinking about what people say. It's definitely second nature for me to think about race and inequities in all areas of my life, not just when something happens. Those events serve as reminders of so much I don't know. Wanting to make a difference worked for me.

What didn't work? Sometimes the conversations got sidetracked and didn't progress in meaningful ways. Sometimes we just spun our wheels, which may be necessary, but it happened less and less as time went on; people said one thing and thought another one. Sometimes only having one or two nonwhite voices was challenging. It would have been great to have had more diverse voices.

What would you do differently? Starting small was a smart idea; it might have been a good idea to have meetings at different times rather than Monday after school. A journey is a journey: things went well some weeks, and some months they didn't—and we are who we are because of the journey we went on. My hope moving forward is that we continue on this journey and don't abandon it because it is so easy to fall back on those habits you've had your whole life.

What advice would I give to staffs at other schools? Stick with it when it gets hard. Commit to an extended amount of time; meaningful work doesn't get done in one session. If you are going to do it, you have to do it within a school culture that is conducive to examining race along with an administrator who is consistent in support. (D. Pritchard, personal communication, March 13, 2013)

Damian, as well as most of the staff, believes taking this journey with his staff changed him forever. What can you take from Damian's words?

Concluding Thoughts From the Principal

Principal Todd Benben may be the most humble man I know. He does not like to draw attention to himself. He does not enable his staff; instead, he empowers them. Below he shares his personal thoughts on the challenging journey his staff engaged in over a number of years.

I am extremely proud of the journey our staff has ventured into over the last few years. A group of adults who were extremely good at what they did decided they wanted to be better than good. Better than great. They wanted to reach and teach everyone, regardless of where they come from, what they have, and what they don't have. They all decided to join the journey and grow themselves as human beings. They started asking tough questions about how they saw situations through their own personal lens in which they see the world and how the culture we create in our classrooms and in our school community can sometimes be obstacles for children of color. By examining our own lenses, we have become a better learning community.

A few years ago some of our staff read Courageous Conversations About Race *(Singleton & Linton, 2006). They thought that the book was so powerful that we needed to do a mandatory book study for all teachers using the book. Some of our staff members, who were extremely disappointed in our African American students' standardized test scores, volunteered to lead the group and began our journey, together. It took multiple years to finish the book, but we persevered and finished. As we finished the book, we have reflected on what has changed since we started the book. We believe that a level of trust formed so that staff could begin to truly share their own stories and their own struggles with race and face up to the white privilege that most of our staff have but were not aware of in our world. Instead of ignoring issues of race, we have begun to face them directly and not let issues go unresolved. We continue the discussions with each other, and some of us have started to reach out to others in our sphere of influence.*

We had the good fortune of having Bonnie Davis and eventually educational consultant Dorothy Kelly support our conversations and help us get better at facilitating and growing our work. They have been instrumental to our guiding our growth and scaffolding our understanding around these difficult but essential conversations. Even though our building scores continue to be at a high level, we have a persistent achievement gap that remains between our African American and white students. The gap has narrowed, but we are not aligned yet, and we will continue our quest to have all our students at or above proficiency. Due to our courageous conversations, our building culture is more inclusive, understanding, and has much more depth to it. I look forward to our continued growth and thoughtful continued conversations!

At North Glendale, we believe all students will learn and grow each and every day. Our daily pledge states that, as learners, we will be cooperative, respectful, responsible, honest—and we will persevere. We take our pledge seriously, and every member of our learning community strives to live our pledge on a daily basis. We have made major strides in building our capacity to be culturally responsive teachers and using what we have learned from each other and from our resources.

Purposeful and engaging work has allowed our learning community to make real progress with our student achievement. Currently, 85 percent of our students are proficient or advanced on the Missouri Assessment Program (MAP) in communication arts, which is a 10 percent improvement over the previous three years. In addition, 83 percent of all our students are proficient or advanced on MAP in math, which is a 12 percent improvement over the previous three years. We are proud that 80 percent of our fifth-grade students scored proficient or advanced on MAP in science. A site called SchoolDigger.com currently ranks our school as the number four elementary school in the state of Missouri. (T. Benben, personal communication, April 16, 2013)

Principal Benben and his staff know the importance of the personal cultural journey, and they continue their work as they strive to evolve as educators in order to reach and teach every child.

Journeying in a Rural/Suburban High School

At a high school in a once-rural Missouri area that is now an outer suburb of St. Louis County, an assistant principal undertook the challenge to increase awareness of the diversity of the student body. She was supported by Terry Harris, the coordinator of educational equity for the district. Jennifer Strausser shares their high school's story.

Three years ago, the staff at Eureka High School, a high school in the Rockwood School District, took on the challenge of increasing our awareness of the diversity of our student body. Because the School District of Rockwood, located in Eureka, Missouri, participates in the voluntary transfer program, we started our efforts with attention to black and white issues.

Without any concrete plan in place, acting on blind faith in ourselves and our motivations, we planned an activity that became one of the most powerful professional development endeavors in which I have ever participated.

The district's voluntary interdistrict coordinating council coordinator and I sat down with a group of ten African American students and taped them answering questions about our school's culture, achievement, and relationships as those topics relate to our black student population. We taped the conversation that was so painfully honest, it brought tears to my eyes.

We then offered a three-part professional learning opportunity to the staff that included two presentations of the video and culminated in a meeting with a student panel, where the teachers were able to ask the same students who were taped questions about how to serve them better.

The fire was lit. What has followed this beautifully simple experience is amazing. Three years later, we have staff and student equity teams. Teachers participate in book studies every year; this year, we did two. We continue to offer diversity-themed professional learning opportunities several times a year.

My latest challenges have been to keep stoking the fire and to widen the scope of our equity work to include other groups of students and teachers who may be gay, of a unique religion, or from other cultures. (J. Strausser, personal communication, April 11, 2013)

Eureka High School's diversity and equity work included the following elements.

- Book studies
  - *The Power of One: How You Can Help or Harm African American Students* by Gail L. Thompson (2010)
  - *The Bus Kids: Children's Experiences With Voluntary Desegregation* by Ira W. Lit (2009)
  - *It's the Little Things: Everyday Interactions That Anger, Annoy, and Divide the Races* by Lena Williams (2002)

- ePLOs (Eureka professional learning opportunities)
  - Three-part video series of roundtable discussion and student panel
  - Parent panel
  - Expert panel (Bonnie Davis)
  - Five days of seminar series by Bonnie Davis about *How to Teach Students Who Don't Look Like You* (Davis, 2012)

- Other efforts
  - Development of the staff equity team with three subcommittees: culture, relationships, and achievement
  - Development of a student equity team

This abbreviated description does not include the extensive work this administration and staff engaged in through numerous book studies, work with equity teams, professional development workshops, and student feedback. First awareness, then a small change in classroom practice, brought about a change in students' attitude and engagement with the lessons. They continue their work and commitment to equity.

Conclusion

Step 6, Engage in a Cultural Literacy Journey, provides the kind of professional development needed to support collaborative conversations focused on the challenging issues of race, equity, and culture. Even though most of the examples in this chapter focus on African American learners, the adult educator journeys would look similar if they were focusing on Latino learners, English learners, Asian learners, American Indian learners, or any other group of learners who do not share the culture of the white educators. The journey works for educators who teach across communities of color, and the strategies work for learners from diverse communities of color. These educators outlined the hard work involved in taking a personal cultural literacy journey, and they shared data showing the payoff for their hard work.

What are some results of their work?

- Teachers are more aware of their implicit biases and are able to talk about race in their classrooms.

- Students are more comfortable with their racial identities.

- The entire staff and students are bound together more closely because they have ventured into territory most dread to tread.

- These educators know their journeys don't end.

- They continue to grow in awareness, each according to an individual path yet more connected to other colleagues and the students, through collaborative conversations.

Reflect on what you read in this chapter. What steps are you willing to take to engage yourself and your staff in a journey of cultural literacy?

As you think back over your journey reading this book, what have you learned?

AFTERWORD

Thank you for your courage, persistence, and commitment to stay with this book until the very end. This book does not have easy answers or a magic bullet. Instead, it asks you to find your own answers in collaborative conversations with others, for when you love your colleagues and convene in a community dedicated to confronting the status quo with fierce conversations, you will be the catalyst for whole-school change. What do you want that change to be?

Reread the following words from the beginning of your journey (found in the introduction) and notice if anything in you has changed:

> Ultimately, this book is about honoring human beings, no matter who they are. It is about the necessity to build relationships in the classroom before we teach the content and continuing to build relationships throughout the teaching of the content. It is about empowering teachers to be able to make decisions about what and when to teach and about empowering learners to join with teachers to question the world and learn together in collaborative inquiry with common curiosity. It is about norming difference and accepting other cultures—in fact, it is about celebrating difference and adjusting our instruction to include cultural practices positively reinforced by other cultures. It is about learning what we don't know we don't know and being willing to examine our impact on each student in our classrooms. It is about the future and learning how to create a better one for all children, growing a more equitable society, and loving those with whom we presently share a learning space. It is about the present and the only time we truly have to make a difference. It is about what you can do now.

In what ways have you grown or changed?

Armed with knowledge of cultural literacy and a greater understanding of how cultural literacy supports the implementation of the Common Core State Standards, and knowing your impact on the learners in your classroom, what are your next steps?

And, finally, thank you for the work you do for *all* children!

REFERENCES AND RESOURCES

Abrams, J. (2009). *Having hard conversations.* Thousand Oaks, CA: Corwin Press.

Adichie, C. (2009, July 18). *The danger of a single story* [Video file]. Accessed at http://www.ted.com/talks/chimamanda_adichie_the_danger_of_a_single_story on May 19, 2014.

Ainsworth, L. (2003). *"Unwrapping" the standards: A simple process to make standards manageable.* Englewood, CO: Lead + Learn Press.

Anderson, K. L. (2010). *Culturally considerate school counseling: Helping without bias.* Thousand Oaks, CA: Corwin Press.

Anderson, K. L., & Davis, B. M. (2012). *Creating culturally considerate schools: Educating without bias.* Thousand Oaks, CA: Corwin Press.

Anderson, L. H. (2005). *Chains.* New York: Atheneum Books for Young Readers.

Anderson, L. H. (2012). *Forge.* New York: Atheneum Books for Young Readers.

Bailey, B. (2001). *Conscious discipline: 7 basic skills for brain smart classroom management.* Oviedo, FL: Loving Guidance.

Bakopoulos, D. (2013, March 22). Straight through the heart. *The New York Times,* p. BR27.

Bellanca, J. A., Fogarty, R. J., & Pete, B. M. (2012). *How to teach thinking skills within the Common Core: 7 key student proficiencies of the new national standards.* Bloomington, IN: Solution Tree Press.

Benben, T. (2013, March 18). *North Glendale Elementary School weekly school bulletin.* Kirkwood, MO: Kirkwood School District.

Blankstein, A. M. (2011). *The answer is in the room: How effective schools scale up student success.* Thousand Oaks, CA: Corwin Press.

Braxton, J. M. (Ed.). (1993). *The collected poetry of Paul Laurence Dunbar.* Charlottesville: University Press of Virginia.

Bronson, P., & Merryman, A. (2010). *NurtureShock: New thinking about children.* New York: Twelve Books.

Brookhart, S. (2008). *How to give effective feedback to your students*. Alexandria, Virginia: Association for Supervision and Curriculum Development.

Brophy, J. E. (1983). Research on the self-fulfilling prophecy and teacher expectations. *Journal of Education*, *75*(5), 631–661.

Brown, B. C. (2012). *Daring greatly: How the courage to be vulnerable transforms the way we live, love, parent, and lead*. New York: Gotham Books.

Browne, J. R., II. (2012). *Walking the equity talk: A guide for culturally courageous leadership in school communities*. Thousand Oaks, CA: Corwin Press.

Brutus, S., & Greguras, G. J. (2008). Self-construals, motivation, and feedback-seeking behaviors. *International Journal of Selection and Assessment*, *16*(3), 282–291.

Burgess, D. (2012). *Teach like a pirate: Increase student engagement, boost your creativity, and transform your life as an educator*. San Diego, CA: David Burgess Consulting.

Calderón, M. E., & Minaya-Rowe, L. (2011). *Preventing long-term ELs: Transforming schools to meet core standards*. Thousand Oaks, CA: Corwin Press.

Campos, D. (2013). *Educating Latino boys: An asset-based approach*. Thousand Oaks, CA: Corwin Press.

Carleton, L., & Marzano, R. (2010). *Vocabulary games for the classroom*. Bloomington, IN: Marzano Research Laboratory.

Cisneros, S. (1984). *The house on Mango Street*. New York: Random House.

CNN Wire Staff. (2012, June 18). *Rodney King dead at 47*. Accessed at www.cnn.com /2012/06/17/us/obit-rodney-king on November 20, 2013.

Collins, S. (2008). *The hunger games*. New York: Scholastic.

Conzemius, A., & O'Neill, J. (2006). *The handbook for SMART school teams*. Bloomington, IN: Solution Tree Press.

Crawford, J. (2012). *Aligning your curriculum to the Common Core State Standards*. Thousand Oaks, CA: Corwin Press.

Culham, R. (2005). *6 + 1 traits of writing: The complete guide for the primary grades*. New York: Scholastic Professional Books.

Davis, B. M. (1988). *A rationale for the reconstruction of the American literary canon*. Unpublished doctoral dissertation, Saint Louis University.

Davis, B. M. (2006). *How to teach students who don't look like you: Culturally relevant teaching strategies*. Thousand Oaks, CA: Corwin Press.

Davis, B. M. (2007). *How to coach teachers who don't think like you: Using literacy strategies to coach across content areas*. Thousand Oaks, CA: Corwin Press.

Davis, B. M. (2009). *The biracial and multiracial student experience: A journey to racial literacy*. Thousand Oaks, CA: Corwin Press.

Davis, B. M. (2012). *How to teach students who don't look like you: Culturally responsive teaching strategies* (2nd ed.). Thousand Oaks, CA: Corwin Press.

Davis, B. M., Kelly, D., Meyer, G., Linton, C., & the Chapel-Hill Carrboro City School District (2011). *The students' six strategies* [Video file]. Accessed at www .schoolimprovement.com/resources/strategy-of-the-week/the-students-six-strategies on May 19, 2014.

Delpit, L. (1995). *Other people's children: Cultural conflict in the classroom.* New York: New Press.

Delpit, L. (1997). Ebonics and culturally responsive instruction. *Rethinking Schools: An Urban Educational Journal, 12*(1), 6–7.

Delpit, L. (2012). *"Multiplication is for white people": Raising expectations for other people's children.* New York: New Press.

Douglass, F. (1987). *Narrative of the life of Frederick Douglass, an American slave.* New York: Signet Classics.

Draper, S. (2006). *Copper sun.* New York: Simon & Schuster.

DuFour, R., DuFour, R., Eaker, R., & Many, T. W. (2006). *Learning by doing: A handbook for professional learning communities at work.* Bloomington, IN: Solution Tree Press.

Dweck, C. S. (2006). *Mindset: The new psychology of success.* New York: Random House.

EngageNY. (n.d.). *Video library.* Accessed at www.engageny.org/video-library?keyword =common+core on May 21, 2014.

Ewald, W. (2002). *The best part of me: Children talk about their bodies in pictures and words.* Boston: Little, Brown.

Fisher, D., & Frey, N. (2013a). *Common Core English language arts in a PLC at work, grades K–2.* Bloomington, IN: Solution Tree Press.

Fisher, D., & Frey, N. (2013b). *Common Core English language arts in a PLC at work, grades 3–5.* Bloomington, IN: Solution Tree Press.

Fisher, D., & Frey, N. (2013c). *Common Core English language arts in a PLC at work, grades 9–12.* Bloomington, IN: Solution Tree Press.

Freire, P. (2000). *Pedagogy of the oppressed* (30th anniversary ed.). New York: Continuum.

Fullan, M. (2008). *The six secrets of change: What the best leaders do to help their organizations survive and thrive.* San Francisco: Jossey-Bass.

Gay, G. (2000). *Culturally responsive teaching: Theory, research, and practice.* New York: Teachers College Press.

Gilligan, C. (1982). *In a different voice: Psychological theory and women's development.* Cambridge, MA: Harvard University Press.

Giouroukakis, V., & Connolly, M. (2012). *Getting to the core of English language arts, grades 6–12: How to meet the Common Core State Standards with lessons from the classroom.* Thousand Oaks, CA: Corwin Press.

Glass, K. T. (2012). *Mapping comprehensive units to the ELA Common Core standards, K–5.* Thousand Oaks, CA: Corwin Press.

Gleason, R. (2007). "Building stronger relationships" (pp. 72–75). Unpublished case study written at the International Education Consortium's Missouri Humanities Program in St. Louis, MO.

Gregory, G. H., & Chapman, C. (2002). *Differentiated instructional strategies: One size doesn't fit all.* Thousand Oaks, CA: Corwin Press.

Haley, A., & Shabazz, A. (1987). *The autobiography of Malcolm X: As told to Alex Haley.* New York: Ballantine.

Hallinan, P. K. (2006). *A rainbow of friends.* Danbury, CT: Ideals Children's Books.

Hamm, M. (2006). *Winners never quit!* New York: HarperCollins.

Hanley, M. S., & Noblit, G. W. (2009). *Cultural responsiveness, racial identity and academic success: A review of literature.* Accessed at www.heinz.org/UserFiles/Library/Culture-Report_FINAL.pdf on February 7, 2014.

Hanover Research Council. (2009). *Recruiting, evaluating, and supporting teacher effectiveness: A review of the literature.* Upper Marlboro, MD: Author.

Hattie, J. A. C. (2009). *Visible learning: A synthesis of over 800 meta-analyses relating to achievement.* New York: Routledge.

Hattie, J. (2012). *Visible learning for teachers: Maximizing impact on learning.* New York: Routledge.

Hattie, J., & Timperley, H. (2007). The power of feedback. *Review of Educational Research, 77*(1), 81–112.

Hayden, R. (1966). Frederick Douglass. In F. Glaysher (Ed.), *Collected poems of Robert Hayden.* New York: Liveright.

Hoffman, M., & Binch, C. (1991). *Amazing grace.* New York: Dial Books for Young Readers.

Honigsfeld, A., & Dove, M. G. (2010). *Collaboration and co-teaching: Strategies for English learners.* Thousand Oaks, CA: Corwin Press.

Howard, G. R. (1999). *We can't teach what we don't know: White teachers, multiracial schools.* New York: Teachers College Press.

Hutchins, D. J., Greenfeld, M. D., Epstein, J. L., Sanders, M. G., & Galindo, C. L. (2012). *Multicultural partnerships: Involve all families.* Larchmont, NY: Eye on Education.

Hyland, K., & Hyland, F. (Eds.). (2006). *Feedback in second language writing: Contexts and issues.* Cambridge, NY: Cambridge University Press.

Jackson, R. (2013). *Teachers trust yourselves and B.Y.O.B.* Accessed at www.mindstepsinc
.com/2013/03/b-y-o-b on May 21, 2014.

Jackson, Y. (2011). *The pedagogy of confidence: Inspiring high intellectual performance in
urban schools.* New York: Teachers College Press.

Jacobs, H. H. (Ed.). (2010). *Curriculum 21: Essential education for a changing world.*
Alexandria, VA: Association for Supervision and Curriculum Development.

Jensen, E. (1998).*Teaching with the brain in mind.* Alexandria, VA: Association for
Supervision and Curriculum Development.

Jensen, E. (2009). *Teaching with poverty in mind: What being poor does to kids' brains
and what schools can do about it.* Alexandria, VA: Association for Supervision and
Curriculum Development.

Johnston, P. H. (2012). *Opening minds: Using language to change lives.* Portland, ME:
Stenhouse.

Kates, B. J. (1992). *We're different, we're the same.* New York: Random House.

Katz, K. (2002). *The colors of us.* New York: Square Fish.

King, M. L., Jr. (1947, January–February). The purpose of education. *The Maroon Tiger.*
Accessed at http://schools.nyc.gov/NR/rdonlyres/33E95C33-A9D1-44D9-AB5C
-30C932CCC2D6/0/MiddleSchoolText.pdf on November 26, 2013.

Knight, J. (2011). *Unmistakable impact: A partnership approach for dramatically improving
instruction.* Thousand Oaks, CA: Corwin Press.

Knight, J. (2013). *High-impact instruction: A framework for great teaching.* Thousand
Oaks, CA: Corwin Press.

Kozol, J. (2012). *Fire in the ashes: Twenty-five years among the poorest children in America.*
New York: Crown.

Krull, K. (2000). *Wilma unlimited: How Wilma Rudolph became the world's fastest
woman.* Boston: Houghton Mifflin Harcourt.

Kung, M. C. (2008). *Why and how do people seek success and failure feedback? A closer
look at motives, methods and cultural differences.* Unpublished doctoral dissertation,
Florida Institute of Technology.

Ladson-Billings, G. (1994). *The dreamkeepers: Successful teachers of African American
children.* San Francisco: Jossey-Bass.

Lemov, D. (2010). *Teach like a champion: 49 techniques that put students on the path to
college.* San Francisco: Jossey-Bass.

Lent, R. C. (2012). *Overcoming textbook fatigue: 21st century tools to revitalize teaching and learning.* Alexandria, VA: Association for Supervision and Curriculum
Development.

Lindsey, R., Robins, K. N., & Terrell, R. D. (2003). *Cultural proficiency: A manual for
school leaders.* Thousand Oaks, CA: Corwin Press.

Linton, C. (2011). *Equity 101—Book 1: The equity framework*. Thousand Oaks, CA: Corwin Press.

Lit, I. W. (2009). *The bus kids: Children's experiences with voluntary desegregation*. New Haven, CT: Yale University Press.

Litwin, E. (2012). *Pete the cat and his four groovy buttons*. New York: HarperCollins.

Locke, E., & Latham, G. (2002). Building a practically useful theory of goal setting and task motivation: A 35-year odyssey. *The American Psychologist, 57*(9), 705–717.

Luque, M. F., & Sommer, S. M. (2000). The impact of culture on feedback-seeking behavior: An integrated model and propositions. *The Academy of Management Review, 25*(4), 829–849.

Martinez-Miller, P., & Cervone, L. (2008). *Breaking through to effective teaching: A walk-through protocol linking student learning and professional practice*. Lanham, MD: Rowman & Littlefield Education.

Marzano, R. J. (2007). *The art and science of teaching: A comprehensive framework for effective instruction*. Alexandria, VA: Association for Supervision and Curriculum Development.

Marzano, R. J. (2009). When students track their progress. *Educational Leadership, 67*(4), 86–87.

Marzano, R. J. (2012). *Becoming a reflective teacher*. Bloomington, IN: Marzano Research Laboratory.

Marzano, R. J., Pickering, D. J., & Pollock, J. E. (2001). *Classroom instruction that works: Research-based strategies for increasing student achievement*. Alexandria, VA: Association for Supervision and Curriculum Development.

Marzano, R. J., Yanoski, D. C., Hoegh, J. K., & Simms, J. A. (2013). *Using Common Core standards to enhance classroom instruction & assessment*. Bloomington, IN: Marzano Research Laboratory.

McCloud, C. (2006). *Have you filled a bucket today?* Northville, MI: Ferne Press.

McEwan-Adkins, E. K., & Burnett, A. J. (2013). *20 literacy strategies to meet the Common Core: Increasing rigor in middle & high school classrooms*. Bloomington, IN: Solution Tree Press.

McIntyre, A. (1997). *Making meaning of whiteness: Exploring racial identity with white teachers*. Albany: State University of New York Press.

McTighe, J., & Wiggins, G. (2013). *Essential questions: Opening doors to student understanding*. Alexandria, VA: Association for Supervision and Curriculum Development.

Mosley, W. (2006). *47*. New York: Little Brown.

Moss, C. M., & Brookhart, S. M. (2012). *Learning targets: Helping students aim for understanding in today's lesson.* Alexandria, VA: Association for Supervision and Curriculum Development.

Muhammad, A. (2009). *Transforming school culture: How to overcome staff division.* Bloomington, IN: Solution Tree Press.

Muhammad, A., & Hollie, S. (2012). *The will to lead, the skill to teach: Transforming schools at every level.* Bloomington, IN: Solution Tree Press.

Myers, W. D. (1999). *Monster.* New York: HarperCollins.

National Governors Association Center for Best Practices & Council of Chief State School Officers. (2010). *Common core state standards for English language arts and literacy in history/social studies, science, and technical subjects.* Washington, DC: Authors. Accessed at www.corestandards.org/wp-content/uploads/ELA_Standards.pdf on May 23, 2014.

Noguera, P. A. (2008). *The trouble with black boys . . . and other reflections on race, equity, and the future of public education.* San Francisco: Jossey-Bass.

Palincsar, A. S. (1986). Reciprocal teaching. In *Teaching reading as thinking.* Oak Brook, IL: North Central Regional Educational Laboratory.

Palmer, P. J. (1998). *The courage to teach: Exploring the inner landscape of a teacher's life.* San Francisco: Jossey-Bass.

Parmer, P., & Steinberg, S. (2008). Locating yourself for your students. In M. Pollock (Ed.), *Everyday antiracism: Getting real about race in schools* (pp. 283–286). New York: New Press.

Perry, T., Hilliard, A., & Steele, C. (2003). *Young, gifted, and black: Promoting high achievement among African-American students.* Boston: Beacon Press.

Polacco, P. (1998). *Thank you, Mr. Falker.* London: Penguin.

Pollock, J. E. (2007). *Improving student learning one teacher at a time.* Alexandria, VA: Association for Supervision and Curriculum Development.

Pollock, J. E. (2012). *Feedback: The hinge that joins teaching and learning.* Thousand Oaks, CA: Corwin Press.

Pollock, J. E., Ford, S. M., & Black, M. M. (2012). *Minding the achievement gap: One classroom at a time.* Alexandria, VA: Association for Supervision and Curriculum Development.

Pollock, M. (Ed.). (2008). *Everyday antiracism: Getting real about race in school.* New York: New Press.

Rath, T., & Reckmeyer, M. (2009). *How full is your bucket? For kids.* New York: Gallup Press.

Reeves, D. B., Wiggs, M. D., Lassiter, C. J., Piercy, T. D., Ventura, S. T., & Bell, B. (2011). *Navigating implementation of the Common Core State Standards.* Englewood, CO: Lead + Learn Press.

Roberts, H. (2011). *Implicit bias and social justice.* Accessed at www.opensocietyfoundations .org/voices/implicit-bias-and-social-justice on May 5, 2014.

Robins, K. N., Lindsey, R. B., Lindsey, D. B., & Terrell, R. D. (2002). *Culturally proficient instruction: A guide for people who teach.* Thousand Oaks, CA: Corwin Press.

Rotner, S. (2009). *Shades of people.* New York: Holiday House.

Rousaki, M. (2008). *Unique Monique.* La Jolla, CA: Kane Miller Books.

Ryan, S., & Frazee, D. (2012). *Common Core standards for high school English language arts.* Alexandria, VA: Association for Supervision and Curriculum Development.

Salazar, R. (2012, May 10). *If you teach or write 5-paragraph essays—Stop it!* [Web log post]. Accessed at www.chicagonow.com/white-rhino/2012/05/if-you-teach-or-write -5-paragraph-essays-stop-it on December 2, 2013.

Schreck, M. K. (2011). *You've got to reach them to teach them: Hard facts about the soft skills of student engagement.* Bloomington, IN: Solution Tree Press.

Schreck, M. K. (2013). *From tired to inspired: Fresh strategies to engage students in literacy.* Bloomington, IN: Solution Tree Press.

Scott, S. (2002). *Fierce conversations: Achieving success at work & in life, one conversation at a time.* New York: Viking Press.

Silver, H. F., Dewing, R. T., & Perini, M. J. (2013). *The core six: Essential strategies for achieving excellence with the Common Core.* Alexandria, VA: Association for Supervision and Curriculum Development.

Singham, M. (1998). The canary in the mine: The achievement gap between black and white students. *Phi Delta Kappan, 80*(1), 9–15.

Singleton, G. (2013). *More courageous conversations about race.* Thousand Oaks, CA: Corwin Press.

Singleton, G., & Linton, C. (2006). *Courageous conversations about race: A field guide for achieving equity in schools.* Thousand Oaks, CA: Corwin Press.

Stewart, V. (2010). A classroom as wide as the world. In H.H. Jacobs, *Curriculum 21: Essential education for a changing world* (pp. 97–114). Alexandria, VA: Association for Supervision and Curriculum Development.

Swartz, R. J. (2007). *Thinking-based learning: Activating students' potential.* Norwood, MA: Christopher-Gorden.

Swartz, R. J., & Parks, S. (1994). *Infusing the teaching of critical and creative thinking into content instruction: A lesson design handbook for the elementary grades.* Pacific Grove, CA: Critical Thinking Press & Software.

Tannen, D. (1990). *You just don't understand: Men and women in conversation.* New York: Ballantine.

Tatum, B. D. (1997). *"Why are all the black kids sitting together in the cafeteria?" and other conversations about race.* New York: Basic Books.

Taylor, Y. (2007). *Growing up in slavery: Stories of young slaves as told by themselves.* Chicago: Chicago University Press.

Thompson, G. L. (2010). *The power of one: How you can help or harm African American students.* Thousand Oaks, CA: Corwin Press.

Tyler, M. (2005). *The skin you live in.* Chicago: Chicago Children's Museum.

Wang, M. C., Haertel, G. D., & Walberg, H. J. (1993). Synthesis of research/what helps students learn? *Educational Leadership, 51*(4), 74–79. Accessed at www.ascd.org/publications/educational-leadership/dec93/vol51/num04/Synthesis-of-Research---What-Helps-Students-Learn¢.aspx on May 8, 2014.

Weisel, E. (2006). *Night.* New York: Hill and Wang.

White House Initiative on Educational Excellence for Hispanic Americans. (2003). *From risk to opportunity: Fulfilling the educational needs of Hispanic Americans in the 21st century—The final report of the President's Advisory Commission on Educational Excellence for Hispanic Americans.* Accessed at www2.ed.gov/about/inits/list/hispanic-initiative/from-risk-to-opportunity.pdf on November 15, 2013.

Wiggins, G. (2010, May 22). *Feedback: How learning occurs.* Accessed at www.authenticeducation.org/ae_bigideas/article.lasso?artid=61 on November 15, 2013.

Wiggins, G., & McTighe, J. (1998). *Understanding by design.* Alexandria, VA: Association for Supervision and Curriculum Development.

Wiggins, G., & McTighe, J. (2005). *Understanding by design* (2nd ed.). New York: Pearson.

Wiggins, G., & McTighe, J. (2012). *The understanding by design guide to advanced concepts in creating and reviewing units.* Alexandria, VA: Association for Supervision and Curriculum Development.

Williams, L. (2002). *It's the little things: Everyday interactions that anger, annoy, and divide the races.* New York: Harcourt.

Yang, G. (2006). *American born Chinese.* New York: First Second Books.

Yetman, N. (2002). *When I was a slave: Memoirs from the slave narrative collection.* Mineola, New York: Dover.

Zobel-Nolan, A. (2009). *What I like about me.* New York: Reader's Digest.

INDEX

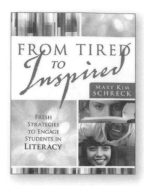

From Tired to Inspired
Mary Kim Schreck
In this Common Core State Standards–aligned book, educators will discover research-based tips and strategies to improve literacy from upper elementary to secondary school classrooms. Topics include teaching close reading and writing, engaging students, making literacy instruction meaningful, and more.
BKF594

Breaking the Poverty Barrier
Ricardo LeBlanc-Esparza and William S. Roulston
Strong leadership, parent involvement, mentoring, data-based intervention, and high expectations are known factors in student success. This book illustrates the specific strategies and critical steps that transformed a school with shockingly low proficiency into a National Showcase School.
BKF476

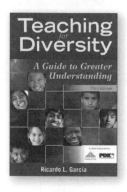

Teaching for Diversity (3rd Edition)
Ricardo L. García
Explore the demographic shifts in American life and schools throughout the late 20th and early 21st centuries, and examine the impact of these shifts on education. This book provides a powerful theoretical framework for thinking about and fostering acceptance of diversity and difference.
BKF400

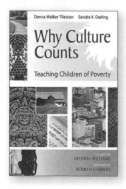

Why Culture Counts
Donna Walker Tileston and Sandra K. Darling
Learn a four-step research-based program for differentiating instruction based on the cultural needs, beliefs, and values of diverse learners. The authors show you how to build teacher background knowledge; plan for differentiation; and differentiate context, content, process, product, and assessment.
BKF255

Solution Tree | Press
a division of
Solution Tree

Visit solution-tree.com or call 800.733.6786 to order.

Wait! Your professional development journey doesn't have to end with the last pages of this book.

We realize improving student learning doesn't happen overnight. And your school or district shouldn't be left to puzzle out all the details of this process alone.

No matter where you are on the journey, we're committed to helping you get to the next stage.

Take advantage of everything from **custom workshops** to **keynote presentations** and **interactive web and video conferencing**. We can even help you develop an action plan tailored to fit your specific needs.

Let's get the conversation started.

Call 888.763.9045 today.

solution-tree.com